The Homing Spirit

THE HOMING SPIRIT

*A Pilgrimage of the Mind,
of the Heart,
of the Soul*

John S. Dunne

CROSSROAD • NEW YORK

1987

The Crossroad Publishing Company
370 Lexington Avenue, New York, N.Y. 10017

Printed in the United States of America

Library of Congress Cataloging in Publication Data

Dunne, John S., 1929–
   The homing spirit.

   1. Spiritual life—Catholic authors.   2. Christian
pilgrims and pilgrimages—Jerusalem.   3. Jerusalem—
Description.   I. Dunne, John S., 1929–   .   II. Title.
BX2350.2.D85   1987   248.4   87-15478
ISBN 0-8245-0837-8

Contents

A Note of Acknowledgment

My first pilgrimage to Jerusalem was in the summer of 1974. My second was in the summer of 1976 when I was writing *The Reasons of the Heart*, given as the Sarum Lectures at Oxford in the fall of 1976. So too I call this second one "a pilgrimage of the heart." During the long "interlude," as I call it here, between the second and the third, I went to the Amazon and wrote *The Church of the Poor Devil* and to Istanbul and wrote *The House of Wisdom*, but I did spend time, as here, just thinking about heart and soul. My last pilgrimage to Jerusalem then was in the summer of 1985. So this book, the outcome of these pilgrimages, is related to my last three books somewhat as my other small book, *Time and Myth*, is to my first three.

My thanks go, first of all, to Sister Marie Goldstein who invited me to participate in the Hope Seminar, the occasion of all three of my journeys to Jerusalem. Also to my fellow participants, Jews and Christians and Muslims, many of whom are quoted here, and especially to Paul Flohr whom I met on my second journey and whose essay on Martin Buber, "The Road to I and Thou," has had considerable influence here. Also, outside of these meetings, to David Daube whose work on New Testament and Rabbinic Judaism, especially his two lectures, "He That Cometh" and "Wine in the Bible," and whose many conversations with me, especially one in 1970 about the "I am" sayings of Jesus, have all been very important here; to Erik

Erikson whose presentation on "The Galilean Sayings and the Sense of 'I'" at the Wellfleet meeting in 1980 has continued to be very stimulating for me; and to Herbert Mason whose work on Al-Hallaj has been very significant for me and who suggested to me Louis Massignon's little piece on "Time in Islamic Thought" which plays a large role here in my thinking on time. Lastly, I am thankful to my teacher Bernard Lonergan, beloved in memory, whose idea of "insight into image" is present everywhere here. I think especially of his lecture, "The Subject," influential here in my thoughts on going from Christ as object to Christ as subject, and also on conversion of mind, of heart, and of soul.

Prologue
The Homing Spirit

Where do you come from? Where are you going? These are the two great questions that are posed in the Gospel of John. If I ask myself these questions, I am asking where home is. I love to think of my life as a journey in time, full of adventures of the soul that become at times voyages and travels of the body as well. When I compare my journeys with those of pilgrims, nevertheless, I can see I have something essential yet to learn. I have gone on my journeys, longing for movement. Pilgrims go on theirs, longing for rest. Where shall I find rest? I have called this book *The Homing Spirit*, thinking of the anguish of not knowing where home is, and the hope and joy of the spirit finding its true home.

It is possible, I learned, to have a direction even though you feel lost and don't know where you are. As I understand it, coming home for the spirit means coming to peace. My own quest of peace, as I tell of it here, takes the form of three pilgrimages to Jerusalem. Maybe calling Jerusalem "the city of peace" is like calling the slum of Calcutta "the city of joy."[1] Still, I did find a way to peace there in conversations with Jews and Christians and Muslims. The way I found was that of "passing over," as I call it, and "coming back," each of us passing over to the others and then coming back again with new insight into our own religion. It is a way I had been following on all my previous journeys but with a difference. Before I had always passed over to others and come back again to myself. My starting and ending point was self, as if self were the home of the spirit. Now I had to go deeper. "Go deep in your own religion," a Sufi sheikh told me. As I heard one of the rabbis in our group sing the Our Father in Hebrew, I realized I had to find a point of rest in myself where I could rest in God, where God dwells in me, and let that be my point of origin and of return. I had to pass over to God in others and come back again to God in myself.

Our loneliness is the place where self opens out upon God, if we take loneliness to be a longing not just for human intimacy but for union with God. The ins and outs of loneliness, finding and losing one another, losing and finding one another, lead us into insight, into realizing God is our heart's desire. "Such are the dealings of Wisdom with the elect soul,"[2] Newman says, thinking of the lonely paths he had to follow in the history of his own religious opinions. We can even come to the point of a conversion, as he did, not a formal change of persuasion maybe but an inner turning to God, an intellectual, a moral, a religious conversion. I felt the need of such a conversion, an inner one, if I was to take part in these meetings of Jews and Christians and Muslims. I had been invited and had agreed to come, but just before I set out upon the first one I decided to let my journey be a pilgrimage. I would turn to God with all my mind and heart and soul.

It is in retrospect that I call this first journey to Jerusalem "a pilgrimage of the mind," for I found peace of mind in the sense of a reality greater than ourselves, in going beyond "I think, therefore I am" to the great "I am" of the burning bush and the Gospel of John. Like perspective in art, the standpoint of self has prevailed in thinking since the time of the Renaissance. Passing over to others and coming back to oneself, it seems to me, is like the transformation of coordinates in the theory of relativity. It means going over to the framework of another observer, another self, and coming back then with new insight to one's own framework. It means becoming conscious of the relativity of one's standpoint, of the relativity of self. The next step then is to become conscious of a reality greater than ourselves, of an "I am" greater than I am. As I was there at Jewish prayer in the synagogue and at home, at Muslim prayer in the mosque and out in open desert, I became conscious of the presence of God. I began to understand Jesus calling God "Abba," almost like Buber calling God "thou." I desired a personal relation with the Lord.

On my second journey, "a pilgrimage of the heart," as I pursued my desire for a personal relation with the Lord, I found peace of heart in restless desire becoming prayer, in contemplative insight into the unquiet "imagination of the heart." The Christian prayer to which I turned from my experience of Jewish prayer and Muslim prayer was "the prayer of the heart," as it is called, where you go from Christ on your lips to Christ in your thoughts to Christ in your heart, only I came at it the other way around, starting with my heart. For I was very conscious of a restlessness of desire, going from one person to another, from one thing to another, always looking for someone or something to fill my heart, a kind of perpetual motion, as if the human heart were like a spinning top, where one image is always changing into another, where everyone and everything become everyone and everything else. Insight into image, I found, insight into the perpetual motion itself, can be a point of repose, of rest in movement, and restless desire can turn into unceasing prayer, the Spirit of Jesus living in your heart.

It is the Lord's Prayer that is the true prayer of the heart, it seems as you enter into the "I and thou" of Jesus with God, or its expansion in John, "I in them and thou in me," or its contraction in the simple cry "Abba!" This stance of prayer, where his Spirit prays in you, where you stand in his place and cry out to his God, became my way of speaking of Father and Son and Holy Spirit as I tried to answer the questions of Jews and Muslims. During the interlude between my second and third journey, I went on further, from prayer of the heart to prayer of the soul. I thought of Paul on the Spirit praying in us when we are at a loss to pray.[3] It is as if God were on both sides of our relation with God. I found here something more elemental than any of the religions, an unconscious reliance on God, the faith that Kafka says is implicit in simply living. From here to conscious faith there is a step, a "leap" Kierkegaard says, as you come consciously and willingly to find support in God.

On my third journey, "a pilgrimage of the soul," I found peace of soul in living in touch with God, in becoming so lonely for God, so lonesome for human beings, that I was able to be caught up in life and light and love. I had been going from an unconscious to a conscious leaning on God, and was coming now to be more and more aware and desirous of God's support. If the human spirit is mind and heart and soul, the Holy Spirit is the indwelling presence of God. Self, I take it, is mind and heart apart from soul, mind as in "I think, therefore I am," heart as in our loneliness for God, our lonesomeness for human beings. On my first journey my mind was opening, on my second my heart was opening, now my soul was opening to presence. I was going from living for my own needs, as Tolstoy says, to living for my soul and remembering God.[4] I was taking courage from Jews and Muslims to say "I am" with Jesus, to go from the "I am I" of autonomy and isolation to the "I am" of life and light and love. Still, I found I could not say "I am" in so strong a way apart from Jesus. I am with him in loneliness as well as in presence.

When I compare my adventures of soul with those of a great mental traveler like Aquinas, I can see still more clearly just what it is I have been learning. My going forth, my passing over, is always from myself, and my return, my coming back, is always to myself. His going forth, on the other hand, as it appears in his Summas, is from God, and his return is to God, and Christ, as he says, is the way. Well, I have been coming to something like that, and my way too is Christ. My passing over is to God in others, really to *one God in three religions*, and my coming back now is to God in myself, not just to loneliness but to indwelling presence. Self has so emerged in thinking and feeling that I cannot abandon its standpoint. It seems to have changed, nevertheless, in passing over, from "I am I" to "I am." Self is indeed like perspective, but in passing over it is a heart as well as an eye, and all lines do converge in its focus, but they diverge again, and this is soul, as they pass on through to infinity.

1

A Pilgrimage of the Mind

I met the unknown! That is what happened, I see now, on my first pilgrimage to Jerusalem. I had to drop all my notions of God and all my notions of myself, and let God reveal God to me, and let God reveal me to me. The very first thing that happened when I arrived, when I was going through customs, was that I saw a happy meeting, a man and a woman and their children. The man had picked up the youngest child, a little girl about two years old, and she was pinching his cheek and saying "Abba, Abba, Abba, Abba."

I knew Jesus used to call God by that name Abba and that he taught his disciples to use it too in prayer, and I knew it was a child's word for Father like Daddy or Papa, but I had never actually heard a child use it and I had never seen the intimacy it could mean, the little girl pinching her father's cheek. I knew Jesus had a relation with God of "unmediated existence"[1] as I came to call it, that there was nothing human to go between him and God, nothing to separate him from God, and so a relation of intimacy, and yet nothing either to serve as a bridge to God, and so at times a relation of distance, as when he cried out "My God, my God, why hast thou forsaken me?"[2] Our own relation with God, if we were to be his followers, had to be different, I had thought, had to be one of "mediated existence," for we had Jesus himself to go between us and God, to be our mediator. Yet now, as I saw the little girl pinching her father's cheek and saying "Abba," I began to see us too entering into that intimacy and distance, entering really into Jesus' own relation, where God is far and near, far as the universe, near as the human heart.

To let God be far and near, to let go of my notions of God, to let go of my notions of myself, to be naked with God, I saw, called for a pilgrimage of the mind. I had to become a pilgrim, far from God, traveling as if in exile, and yet near to God, dwelling as if at home. I had to become a "mental traveler,"[3] as in William Blake's poem, going backwards in time, for I had to go from being a disciple at secondhand, at twenty centuries remove from Jesus, to being a disciple at firsthand. As it was, I was invited to Jerusalem to participate in a conversation of Jews and Christians and Muslims, a traveling conversation in which we would visit holy places of the three religions. I was called upon to "pass over," as I thought of it, to enter sympathetically, into Judaism and Islam, and then to "come back" again with new insight into Christianity. Yet the secret of passing over, at least for me, I saw now, was to enter more deeply into Christianity, to enter into the nakedness of Jesus with God.

When I do enter into his relation with God, I found, when I stand where he stands, then he disappears from in front of me and I find myself alone with God. There is a moment of loneliness, I mean, when there seems to be nothing to separate me from God and yet nothing either to unite me with God. But then there comes a moment when it is I who disappear, when I seem to understand "it is no longer I who live, but Christ who lives in me."[4] I go from loneliness to being caught up in a reality greater than myself.

The Test of Loneliness

"I am happy here," a Bedouin told us, living in the Sinai desert, "but if I saw Jerusalem I would not be happy anymore." Our traveling conversation of Jews and Christians and Muslims took us into the Sinai, and there we met this friendly and helpful man who had never been outside of the desert, and so we invited him to come back with us and visit Jerusalem. His "No" seemed wise to me. I thought of the story of the Well at the World's End,[5] how its water is not for the happy but for the unhappy. Jerusalem too, it seemed to me, is not for those who are in agreement with their world, like this happy man of the desert, but for those who are searching for something, like us Jews and Christians and Muslims. Yet as I pondered his words the more, I thought I too should take them to heart. "I am happy here," he said. "I am in pursuit of happiness," I said to myself. "If I saw Jerusalem I would not be happy anymore," he said. "If I saw Jerusalem," I said to myself, "I would have to embrace not only the joy, when God seems near at hand, but also the sorrow of life, when God seems far away."

To be in pursuit of happiness, as I was, is very different from being happy, as he was. I had gone through loss, before ever I came to the Holy Land, and it had left me feeling very alone, and I was seeking on my pilgrimage to be cured of my sorrow. I was like all those in the story who were saying "I must drink of the Well at the World's End." It was peace that I was looking for, the peace that is spoken of in the Gradual Psalms sung by pilgrims on the way to Jerusalem, the peace that is invoked in everyday greeting, *shalom* in Hebrew, *salam* in Arabic. If I could find peace, I would be cured of sorrow. Yet to see Jerusalem, as I began to realize, is to see beyond the object of one's seeking. It is to see beyond even the pursuit of happiness. "This is not Jerusalem,"[6] pilgrims have said in the past, disappointed by the contrast between seeking and finding. To find peace, I realized, I had to be able to say without regret, "This is Jerusalem."

I was meditating on the words "and his will is our peace"[7] (I find them in my diary on the day we set out for the Sinai). I was thinking peace comes of remembering God and unpeace of forgetting God. My pilgrimage was to be an exercise in remembering God, a calling of God to mind, and thus truly a pilgrimage of the mind. That is how I expected to find peace. I came upon an unknowing in myself, though, almost as in the words of Jesus weeping over Jerusalem, "If thou hadst known, even thou, at least in this thy day, the things which belong unto thy peace!"[8] It was as if the words were addressed to me rather than to Jerusalem. If I had known, even I, at least in this my day, the things which belong unto my peace! My unknowing came out as an uncertainty, even in my bearing. I was "going into the morrow," one of my fellow pilgrims observed, but was "uncertain of wanting to go there." I was seeking peace, pursuing happiness, but was unwilling as yet to embrace the sorrow as well as the joy of life.

I was going through what I have come to know as "the test of loneliness," as in the story of Hezekiah where it is said "God left him to himself, in order to try him and to know all that was in his heart."[9] God does leave us to ourselves at times, it seems, in order to try us and to know all that is in our hearts, and not only for God to know, it seems to me now, but also for us to know. What is in our hearts? What is in my heart? That is my question now as I relive my experience in recollection. *What is it to know the heart?* "For the heart guides the steps," a pilgrim has said, "and has intentions too deep for the mind to grasp at once."[10]

Thinking of the heart, I think of a Bedouin girl we saw in the Sinai, playing on a wooden flute, leading a flock of goats. We met her as we were going on the old pilgrim's walk to Mount Sinai. She played the flute for us, but from a distance and without lifting her veil. She must have been about thirteen years old. As we walked out of the wadi and came in sight of Saint Catherine's Monastery and Mount Sinai, she waved goodbye to us and turned back, playing her flute, with all the goats following. She was like the heart, playing, guiding the steps, but never lifting her veil, never revealing herself. It is only in retrospect, it seems, that the mind can grasp the intentions of the heart, only after the steps have already been taken. That she turned back into the wadi and did not go with us to

Mount Sinai was like the man refusing to go with us to Jerusalem. Maybe she too could have said "I am happy here," and maybe also, speaking for the heart, "If I went with you I would not be happy anymore."

To be a pilgrim is to have "the wishing heart," though, and I certainly had it, seeking peace and the cure of my sorrow, and when you enter upon a journey like this, as one of my fellow pilgrims said to me, the journey takes you. So there can be no turning back. As I thought the more on the girl playing the flute, nevertheless, I took her also to heart. There was wisdom, it seemed, in her turning back. What it was I would learn by going on. I would learn at Gebel Musa, Mount Moses as the Bedouin call Mount Sinai. I knew the story, how Moses was keeping the flock of his father-in-law, and led his flock to the west side of the wilderness, and came to this mountain, the mountain of God. It was like the girl keeping her flock and leading it here, except that Moses went on instead of turning back. And here he met the unknown, the burning bush, a bush that was on fire but was not consumed. "I will turn aside and see this great sight," he said, "why the bush is not burnt." That was his fateful choice, to turn aside and see. "When the Lord saw that he turned aside to see," the story goes on, "God called on him out of the bush, 'Moses, Moses!'"[11]

That is what might happen to me, if I went on, God might call me by name, and that, I thought, is what did happen, call echoing call, as it seemed, God calling to me and me calling to God. We climbed Mount Sinai at dawn, and then climbed down again in the afternoon, and then at night (I find in my diary), as I walked with one of my fellow pilgrims in the moonlight in the small wadi where we were camping, I told her the whole pilgrimage for me was a renewal of my sense of a call. It was a remembering of God, a calling of God to mind, and thus a being remembered, a being called myself. It was a choosing and thus a being chosen. My uncertainty, my "going into the morrow" and being "uncertain of wanting to go there," was indecision, I began to think, a hesitancy to commit myself. I had to come somehow to a turning point, a conversion of the mind, like the moment described in the diary of Dag Hammarskjold when he says, "For all that has been — Thanks! To all that shall be — Yes!"[12]

There is a loneliness about "going into the morrow" that makes you "uncertain of wanting to go there." It is the loneliness of having a past and a future, of being far and near, far from yourself in the past and the future and near yourself in the present. God then too is far and near, and this is "the test of loneliness." To pass the test, it seems, you have to say "Thanks!" for the past and "Yes!" to the future. You have indeed to embrace the sorrow as well as the joy of life, for it is the sorrow that turns us away from the past and the future, the pain of loss. If there is wisdom in turning away from Jerusalem, like the man saying "I am happy here," or in turning back from Mount Sinai, like the girl playing the flute, it is the wisdom of living in the present. That is the wisdom of the desert, where God is always near, where you are always near yourself.

I felt far from God and far from myself, as we came back from the Sinai to Jerusalem, and especially as we traveled along the Dead Sea, almost as if there were, in the words of a friend, "something standing between myself and my sense of well-being," a distance of some kind between me and the peace I was seeking. That something, that distance, I think now in retrospect, was time, the past and the future. I had not yet been able to say "Thanks!" for the past and "Yes!" to the future, and so I was not yet able to live in the present, or better, as I think of the Bedouin I saw praying in the desert, touching their heads to the ground, at sunrise, at noon, at sunset, I was not yet able to live in the presence of God. As I think of all this, I can understand what a long pilgrimage of the mind Martin Heidegger had to travel in our century from his early thinking in *Being and Time*, where time is seen as coming between us and ourselves, to his late thinking in *Time and Being*, where time seems to become transparent to eternity.[13] That had to be my pilgrimage too, from time to eternity, from living in a past and a future to living in an eternal presence.

In thinking, Heidegger says, the far becomes near and the near becomes far. God becomes near as I think of God being far, and I become near myself as I think of being far from myself. So it was then, as I brought my own memories to Jerusalem, a place of memory, and so it is now, as I remember memory. I go from living in the past and in the future to living in the present, and that "something standing between myself and my sense of well-being" seems to vanish, the distance of the past and the future, the pain of loss, and all that remains is the instant, the now. "What is the instant?" I ask myself. "It is a breeze of joy blown by pain," Al-Hallaj says, a breeze of joy I am feeling now blown by pain I was feeling then. The far becomes near, that is, and yet the near becomes far, "and Wisdom is waves which submerge, rise, and fall, so that the instant of the Sage is black and obscured."[14] God becomes far as I think of God being near, and I become far from myself as I think of being near myself.

God is far and near, therefore, at least in thinking, and I am far and near. What becomes then of the instant, the moment of joy? "The instant is a pearl-bearing shell, sealed at the bottom of the ocean of the human heart," Al-Hallaj says; "tomorrow, at the rising tide of Judgement, all shells will be cast on the beach; and we shall see if any pearl emerges from them." Here is an answer to my question, "What is in our hearts? What is in my heart?" I think of the parable of the pearl. "Again, the kingdom of heaven is like a merchant in search of fine pearls," Jesus says, "who, on finding one pearl of great value, went and sold all that he had and bought it."[15] I think also of the poem *Pearl* about a man who has lost his little daughter, his pearl, and who meets her again in a dream. That is what I sought in Jerusalem as a place of memory, as a wailing wall, an empty tomb, a stepping stone to heaven—I hoped to find again what I had lost. I think also, though, of the novel *The Pearl* by John Steinbeck, where the pearl is cast back again into the depths of the sea. Should I have left the pearl, undisturbed by thinking, at the bottom of my heart?

No, if the pearl is "the instant of divine certainty perceived in the heart,"[16] then it may be found in thinking, at least in thinking that is heart-searching. It is true, the instant is first of all "the instant of anguish," like the grain of sand around which the pearl is secreted. It is only in time, as the grain is surrounded by layer after concentric layer of nacre, that it becomes the timeless moment of joy. The anguish of being left to myself, the loneliness I felt in my loss, was as if my heart were being searched. God tries us by loneliness, I believe now, as he seemed to be doing then, to search our heart and to invite us also into the heart-searching, call echoing call, search following search. The experience of the heart being searched is pain, but it turns into joy as it becomes the experience of being known by God. The sense of being known then is "the instant of divine certainty perceived in the heart."

I was learning something in Jerusalem that I had not learned in the Sinai, "the instant of anguish," the significance of pain. There is knowing in being known. I wrote in my diary the words of Jesus, "He who finds his life will lose it, and he who loses his life for my sake will find it,"[17] circling the words "for my sake." Seeing Jerusalem was significant, seeing Jerusalem, that is, as a pilgrim rather than as a tourist. That to me was the meaning of "for my sake." Seeing as a pilgrim meant taking my own loss as "a shock of grace," as "a severe mercy." Seeing as a tourist would have meant taking it only as a personal matter having nothing to do with what I was seeing. As it was, "He who finds his life will lose it" was my experience, "and he who loses his life for my sake will find it" was my hope. As Louis Massignon says, "The instant of anguish is essentially prophetic . . . it announces the final stopping of the pendulum of our vital pulse on the tonic of its scale, on the 'place of its salvation.'"[18] Taking it as "a shock of grace" means living towards grace, taking it as "a severe mercy" means living towards mercy. Or better, it means living under grace, living under mercy. "It is not a fragment of duration," Massignon concludes, "it is beyond doubt a divine 'touch' of theologal hope, which transfigures our memory forever." That is what I was seeking, bringing my own loss to Jerusalem, a hope that transfigures memory. Yet I did not go to the Holy Sepulchre on that first pilgrimage (I did on my later pilgrimages), even though the empty tomb is the place where Christians have traditionally gone to find hope. I did not go, I suppose, because the tomb is empty, because Jesus is not there. "Why do you seek the living among the dead?"[19] Instead, by taking my loss as a stroke of grace, by taking it as a stroke of mercy, I hoped to find grace, to find mercy. By going through my own loss hopefully and willingly, by going *here*, in Jerusalem, through the *now*, "the instant of anguish," I would go with Jesus through death to life.

I had known the Christian mystery was one of life and death, of going through death to life, but until now, until my own "instant of anguish," I had thought our going through was symbolic during life and real only at the hour of our death. As Jung once said, after an encounter with death, "I only know now how real these things are."[20] I only know now, after going through loss, how real the passage through death can be during life. I have passed through, if indeed I have, by leaving all I had, or rather *all I had not*, to follow Jesus in death and in life. Have I passed through? I have entered into the Christian mystery, but have I made it through to life? Or have I become stranded in death? Here is the peril of the Christian mystery. In order to pass through death to life you have to let go of everyone and everything, not only what you have but also what you do not have, but letting go of what you do not have is like dying without having lived—to do it you have to trust in God giving everyone and everything back to you again in a new life, in a new relationship. You have to believe, without knowing how, that you will live.

A "Yes!" and a "Thanks!", a hope that transfigures memory — that is what it means to believe that you will live. I think again of the man who has lost his pearl, his little daughter, and who meets her again in a dream. I had a dream like that in Jerusalem. I find it in my diary just before the words, "He who finds his life will lose it, and he who loses his life for my sake will find it." Finding and losing, therefore, losing and finding, that is the meaning of my dream. Yet what is it to find again the life you have lost? Is it to find happiness? Or is it to find something more than happiness? It is to find something more, I believe now, to find a peace that embraces joy and sorrow. That is not happiness pure and simple. It is conscious well-being, and you come to this consciousness by finding and losing, by losing and finding your well-being.

Is loss then inevitable? No, "the instant of anguish" can occur apart from any experience of loss. The stroke of grace, the stroke of mercy is "perceived as an instant of anguish," according to Massignon, "without duration but endowed with a variety of mental colors."[21] It can be an ecstasy of joy or an ecstasy of pain, an ecstasy of love or an ecstasy of fear. In the experience of loss "the instant of anguish," otherwise "without duration," is endowed with duration and becomes part of our experience of living in time, of having a past and a future. As long as we live only in the present "the instant of anguish" has only a "hidden persistence," is "like a germ of hidden immortality, buried at the bottom of the heart." That is what I was seeing in the Sinai, the happiness of those who live in the present. Once we enter into time and become conscious of having a past and a future "the instant of anguish" can no longer be hidden. That is what I was feeling in Jerusalem, the loneliness of those who live in time.

To be or not to be in time, therefore, that is the question. "Only one who lives not in time but in the present is happy,"[22]

Ludwig Wittgenstein says, and I could see the truth of that in the desert, in the man saying "I am happy here, but if I saw Jerusalem I would not be happy anymore," in the young girl leading her flock and playing on her wooden flute. Yet time is "the lighting-up of the self-concealing,"[23] Heidegger says, and I could feel the truth of that in Jerusalem, in the heart-searching, in the pain of loss and of loneliness. I was too far into the consciousness of time to be able to turn my back on the past and the future and simply live in the present. I had to find a future that transfigures the past, a hope that transfigures memory. Yet I had to let go of the past and the future that I knew, to let go of the pain of loss. I had somehow to forget.

What is it to forget the pain of loss? One night I went with a Muslim friend to a small mosque in the Old City of Jerusalem. There I saw young Sufis dancing and chanting "Allah, Allah, Allah, Allah." I saw how "the disappearance of the instant of anguish could leave the heart with a kind of 'rhythmic impulse' and an enduring promise of plenitude, the beginning of a Wisdom situated outside of time."[24] The dancing was simple, like jumping; the chanting was rhythmical, like breathing; the remembering of God was a forgetting of all else. I had learned from Augustine to remember God by remembering all else, by bringing my life to mind, by heart-searching. So it was not easy for me to enter into what they were doing, to remember by forgetting. If "the instant of anguish" sank to the bottom of my heart while they were dancing and chanting, it rose again to the surface when I came back again to myself. The "rhythmic impulse" ceased, and everyone sat down, and mint tea was served, and the mood for me, though not for them, was broken. I was throbbing already with my own heartbeat, with my own pain, while they were still pulsing with the thought of God.

I could not forget memory, I learned, but I could "remember forgetfulness,"[25] as Augustine says, I could remember what it is to be so absorbed in God as to forget the pain of loss. The young Sufis chanting "Allah, Allah, Allah, Allah" are an image to me of forgetting; the child pinching her father's cheek and saying "Abba, Abba, Abba, Abba" is an image of remembering. I had to find a forgetting that is also a remembering, a remembering that is also a forgetting. After we stood up, and saluted one another warmly with a handclasp and a kiss on the hand, we came out of the mosque, and the young Sufis surrounded me, knowing I was a Christian, and began to ask me questions about Jesus. It came to me then that Jesus is my answer, my remembering and my forgetting. "So you have sorrow now," he says, "but I will see you again and your hearts will rejoice, and no one will take your joy from you."[26] Meanwhile, my friend who brought me, seeing the questions go on, said "Come, let us go now."

The Bread of the Coming One

When we went on then to Galilee, some days later, it was as if to meet Jesus, as if we were responding to his promise, "I will go before you to Galilee."[27] I thought of an old man who once asked me, many years ago, "Have you met Jesus?" Now, I thought, I will. Here comes my remembering and my forgetting. There is a forgetting that comes of sheer joy, like that of a woman who has given birth, who "no longer remembers the anguish, for joy that a child is born into the world." That is the forgetting I was seeking. It is a forgetting that comes of remembering, of remembering joy. And that is the remembering I was seeking, the joy of the man alive, of Jesus risen from the dead. It sounds like the pursuit of happiness all over again, but it was really something more, a going through sorrow to joy, as in his words, "you will be sorrowful, but your sorrow will turn to joy."[28] I was seeking not simply to forget but to "remember forgetfulness," not simply to remember but to "remember memory," as if I were responding to his command, "Do this in memory of me."[29]

I was seeking a hope, a memory, a hope that transfigures memory. I was seeking a presence. It is true, when "I summon up the remembrance of things past," as Shakespeare says, and am "dreaming on things to come,"[30] I retain in my mind only images of "things past," only images of "things to come." Still, hope is really hope, and memory is really memory, and if I remember hope, I am remembering joy, and if I "remember memory," the things I remember are reaching me and happening to me. So if a hope transfigures my memory, a faith ("that Christ may dwell in your hearts by faith"),[31] then I retain not only images of the past, not only images of the future, but more than that a presence of hope, a presence of memory, really a presence of mind. I retain not only an image of Christ, that is, but a sense of his presence. So it is that joy dwells in my heart, and I am able at last to say "Yes, I have met Jesus."

Joy comes and goes, nevertheless, and for all my presence of mind I cannot seem to make it come when I wish. "A little while, and you will see me no more," Jesus says; "again, a little while, and you will see me."[32] Joy goes when he goes, it seems, when I am alone, as I was in Jerusalem, and God seems far away, and joy comes when he comes, when I meet him, as I hoped in Galilee, and God seems near at hand. I was thinking of him in Jerusalem too, and my feeling that I was alone was like his and my feeling that God was far away, "but then joy is never in our power," C. S. Lewis says, and we cannot make it come at will, though "anyone who has experienced it will want it again."[33] It is the experience of joy, the feeling, that seems never to be in our power. Joy may dwell, Christ may dwell in my heart by faith, but I cannot summon up the feeling of joy, I cannot summon up the sense of his presence, as "I summon up the remembrance of things past." It is only when hope jogs my memory, transfigures my memory, that joy comes, that he comes, for joy belongs to conscious well-being. It is a taste, a foretaste, an aftertaste of heart's desire.

As I pondered the old man's question, "Have you met Jesus?," as I took it to heart and let it speak to me of heart's desire, I realized I could not bring about the meeting with Jesus myself, I could not pass from sorrow to joy simply by my own presence of mind. Still, if "joy is never in our power and pleasure often is," if joy is "more desirable than any other satisfaction," as Lewis says, I could choose joy over pleasure, I could choose joy over any other satisfaction. I could ask God for my heart's desire. I could ask, as in the Lord's Prayer, for "daily bread," or better, for "the bread from heaven," or better still, for "the bread of the Coming One."[34]

One evening at sunset, as I sat by the Sea of Galilee, I was meditating on the Beatitudes, on the poor in spirit, those who mourn, the meek, those who hunger and thirst for justice, the merciful, the pure in heart, the peacemakers, those who suffer for justice, on Jesus calling them "blessed" and saying "theirs is the kingdom of heaven."[35] I felt drawn by the purity and simplicity of following Jesus, almost as if he found me there meditating and said "Follow me." I was touched by joy then. It was the turning point. It was "the bread of the Coming One." It was a taste of heart's desire, I mean, a foretaste of Someone or Something still to come, an aftertaste of Someone or Something already come. I felt twenty centuries drop away between me and Jesus. I felt I was no longer a disciple at secondhand but a disciple at firsthand like Peter and John and Mary Magdalene. I thought again of the old man and his question, and I asked myself "Have you met Jesus?" and I found I could say "Yes!"

I have wondered if this was only an aesthetic and not a religious experience. It was only a taste, a foretaste, an aftertaste. Still, it was of heart's desire, of heart speaking to heart. "There is no disciple at second hand," Soren Kierkegaard says, and everyone who believes is a disciple at firsthand, for the gap that faith is always crossing is not merely a gap of time but of eternity in time. It is, he says, "the beginning of eternity."[36] I did

have a distinct feeling of crossing a gap of time, of twenty
centuries dropping away, and yet it was indeed "the beginning
of eternity" for me, a stirring of heart's desire, of the deep
yearning in human loneliness that is the eternal in us. It was a
feeling of heart speaking to heart across time, across time past
and time future in a way that only eternity can span time. It
was a taste of presence as well as a foretaste of "things to come"
and an aftertaste of "things past," a presence of hope, "the substance of things hoped for," a presence of memory, "the evidence
of things not seen," the presence of mind that can be called
"faith."[37] Or it became all this, I think now, as I took it to heart.

Here was my remembering and my forgetting, in taking it to
heart, in choosing joy over pleasure, in choosing it also over
pain rather than holding on to sadness, in choosing it over
settled happiness even, to follow joy wherever it would lead. I
was in Nazareth the next day at the place where Charles de
Foucauld lived for three years before going to live in the Sahara
Desert. Here was someone who took "Follow me" to heart. I
came across his *prière d'abandon*, his meditation on the last words
of Jesus, "Father, into thy hands I commit my spirit."[38] He
wanted that to be the prayer not only of the last but of every
instant of his life, to let every day be "the beginning of eternity,"
the ever-recurring moment of surrender, of abandon to the will
of God. I wanted it to be my prayer too, for there is a peace, I
could see, almost a settled happiness after all, in that taking to
heart, in that choosing, in that abandon. "I am happy,"
Foucauld wrote from the desert, "and I lack nothing."

There is a peace in presence of mind, or there can be, even
though joy comes and goes. It is the peace that comes of living
on "the bread of the Coming One," of welcoming joy when it
comes, of awaiting it when it goes. No doubt, there is a presence of mind that comes simply of self-control, of maintaining
self-command in emergency, in danger, in difficult situations of
all kinds, being able to say the right thing, to do the right thing,

being unshaken and calm and ready. But there is a deeper presence of mind that comes of self-surrender, of abandon to the will of God. Self-control is a restraint exercised over impulse; abandon is a yielding to impulse. Abandon to the will of God, though, is a yielding to the heart's longing, to the deep yearning of the human spirit, a choosing of heart's desire over every other impulse and emotion and desire.

I felt near God and near my heart's desire as we came back then from Galilee to Jerusalem, as we traveled along the Jordan. "I saw in my mind's eye, and sensed in my heart," a friend once wrote to me, "this floating form of God whispering in my ear." I cannot say I visualized God in so vivid a manner, but I did have a sense of communing with God and of discerning the movements of my heart. If presence of mind is in being present to oneself, it can deepen nevertheless into being in the presence of God, and in that presence what I am calling "heart's desire" can be discerned as lasting desire hidden in every passing desire, as longing "for the food which endures to eternal life" hidden in every longing "for the food which perishes."[39] That deepening takes place as one's day-to-day conversation with oneself turns into a conversation with God, as soliloquy gives way to prayer. I can see that presence of mind in my diary over the years, and I know it often became for me the presence of God, but it seemed I could sustain it more after this experience in Galilee. I could find a sustenance in it that was an answer somehow to my loneliness.

For if presence of mind means having one's wits about one, it comes to mean, as it deepens, having all the persons about one who belong to one's life, all the "interceding witnesses" of one's life, as Massignon calls them, living and dead. It means coming to feel their presence as one feels the presence of God. So it was for Massignon himself at his conversion or return to faith when, as he said, he received the "visitation of the Stranger," when God visited him and penetrated his heart, and he found himself, a "witness of the instant," linked with God, the "Witness of the Eternal."[40] So it was for me too, I realize now, when I received my own "visitation of the Stranger" in Galilee, when I had my encounter with "the Coming One." I felt, or I came to feel in that presence of mind, the presence of all those who belong to my life, and especially the ones I had lost, thinking at the time of Jesus praying "for those whom thou hast given me,"[41] and thus becoming linked myself with the "Witness of the Eternal."

Everyone who belongs to my life is far and near, it seems, as God is far and near, as I myself am far and near, in my presence of mind. It is, I suppose, because the far becomes near and the near becomes far in thinking. And yet no one goes lost who belongs to my life, I want to believe, for my own consciousness of time, the "witness of the instant," is linked with a greater consciousness of eternity, the "Witness of the Eternal." Maybe that is what Jesus is talking about in his argument with the Sadducees about resurrection of the dead, when he says God "is not God of the dead, but of the living," and especially when he adds, according to Luke, "for all live to him."[42] If all are alive to God, and if I participate somehow in that eternal consciousness, then all are alive to me and none are lost to me. All I have to show for this, though, is the awareness I have, the presence of mind in which I feel their presence or I feel they are far and near. It is as if I were calling God to witness as in an oath, and not just to the truth of my words or of my intended deeds but to the very truth of my thoughts, witness attesting to witness.

If I have to call God to witness, it is as if my own witness, my own consciousness, were not enough. There is indeed a "unity of witness," as Al-Hallaj calls it, a union with God, that I am seeking, calling on God to be present, for if all who are alive to me are alive to God, then all are truly alive. Really, it is not an oath I am taking so much as an affirmation I am making of

God's presence, as in the words of Jesus, "Do not swear at all" and "Let what you say be simply Yes or No."[43] All I can do is bear witness to my own presence of mind, to my own presence to myself and to God's presence to me and to the presence of all who belong to my life. I can only let the "I am" of my presence of mind give way to the "I am" of God's presence, as perhaps Al-Hallaj is doing when he says "I am the truth," as perhaps Jesus is doing when he says "I am" in the Gospel of John, where "I am" means "God is here."

I was meditating on the "I am" sayings of Jesus during my last days in Jerusalem after returning from Galilee. "I am" means "The Divine Majesty itself is here," according to David Daube, in the Gospel of John and also in the Jewish Passover liturgy. Also *Aphiqoman*, the name of the piece of bread set aside at the beginning and eaten at the end of this liturgy, means "the Coming One." It was this bread, most likely, that Jesus gave to his disciples at the Last Supper, saying "This is my body." He was saying "This is me," that is, or "I am the Coming One."[44] All I was learning from Judaism about the presence of God (the Shekinah), it seemed, and all I was learning from Islam about living in the presence of God, was coming together for me in what I was learning about presence of mind. There is an "I am" that expresses presence of mind, the "I am" that everyone can say, as in "I think, therefore I am," and there is a greater "I am" that only God can say, as in the burning bush in the Sinai, and there is a fading of the one into the other, of presence of mind into the presence of God, in the coming of the Coming One.

"I am and no other," the words occurring in the Passover liturgy, like "I am" in Exodus and in the Gospel of John, are words expressing the presence of God. Yet the words are pronounced by human beings. So they imply a union with God, indeed a "unity of witness" in which human beings can speak for God. When Jesus says "I am" in the Gospel of John, he seems to be speaking out of this union, this unity of witness attesting to witness, and when I enter into his relationship with

God, I am conjoining my own witness, my own consciousness with his. It is true, my attempt to join him can be merely an exercise in remembering his words, where memory brings no comfort, is only images as in a mirror, and I find myself longing for real presence. Or it can be instead an exercise in memory transfigured by hope, as it was for me in Jerusalem, where words act, where memory is more like waking consciousness than it is like dreaming.

It is hope that makes the difference or really, as I came to see soon afterwards, a combination of hope and willingness, as when a person is willing to die and yet hopes to live. Say I am sick and am facing death. If I am willing to die and do not hope to live, I will go quietly to my death, but if I do hope to live and am unwilling to die, I will fight death to the end. What if I am willing to die and yet hope to live? Then I may well recover from my illness. At any rate, the combination of hope and willingness is very healing and life-giving. It is what Kierkegaard calls "faith." Willingness without hope he calls "infinite resignation."[45] I found myself at the end, during my last days in Jerusalem, confronted with a choice between "faith" and "infinite resignation" in facing my own past and future. After all I had seen and felt I had to go the way of willingness, of saying "Yes," and it did feel very much like a willingness to die. Still, I could hope to live, to recover somehow the life I had lost. The presence of mind that comes of hope seemed much more vivid, much more a real presence, than that of willingness without hope.

It was as if the life I was hoping for were given to me already in hope itself or in the presence of mind that comes about through hope. "I am, be not afraid,"[46] the words of Jesus walking on the water, speak to hope as well as to fear, for where there is hope there is also fear and where there is fear there is also hope. What do I fear? What may I hope? I fear being alone. I may hope God will be with me, I may hope in "I am." When Jesus says "Come" then to Peter, to me, to walk to him across the water, he is inviting me to trust in that presence. I think of the jokes we made by the Sea of Galilee about walking on the water. If I do trust nonetheless, as I was doing now in Jerusalem, I am choosing "faith" over "infinite resignation," I am choosing joy over grief. I can say, with Foucauld, "Jesus is the Master of the impossible."[47]

The impossible becomes possible, I mean, when I enter into the presence of God, into the consciousness of "I am." It is always heart's desire that seems impossible in a life, impossible of attainment. "I dare not believe," Hammarskjold said on the eve of his own turning point, "I do not see how I shall ever be able to believe: that I am not alone."[48] Here is heart's desire, the longing in our loneliness, the deep yearning for union and communion, and beyond here is faith, while being willing to live in longing and loneliness to hope nonetheless for union and communion, while embracing sorrow as well as joy in life to choose joy nonetheless over sorrow. I am not alone, I believe now, for God is with me, for all the persons who belong to my life are with me, even the ones I have lost, for I can feel God's presence, their presence — I am caught up in a reality greater than myself, an "I am" greater than I am. In fact, "I am," when I say it, means "I am not alone."

To know the heart, I conclude, is to go beyond "I think, therefore I am," *to go beyond self-consciousness to the consciousness of a reality greater than myself.* It is only when my presence of mind heightens and deepens, it seems, that I come to understand heart's desire, for the heart remains divided as long as it is left in the darkness of mere self-consciousness. I cannot discern heart's desire, that is, from the many impulses and emotions and desires that it pervades, from the heartburning of jealousy, from the heartache of sorrow, from the heartsickness of despondency, except in the light of God's presence. To know the heart thus is to discern the one in the many. It is to know God in my heart.

It is to go beyond the heartbreak that can take away self-command and presence of mind. It is to find peace of mind, like Augustine in his *Confessions*, by making contact with something that goes deeper than self-command. I think of Alcoholics Anonymous speaking of "a Power greater than ourselves," much as I am speaking of "a reality greater than myself." I think of their experience of "bottoming out," going down one side and coming up the other side of a V, becoming "powerless over alcohol," finding life has "become unmanageable," coming "to believe that a Power greater than ourselves could restore us to sanity," and choosing "to turn our will and our lives over to the care of God as we understood Him."[49] My own experience, I can see, has been very similar, going down one side and coming up the other side of a V of loss and recovery, going through a heightening and deepening of presence of mind. For me too it has meant coming to believe that a power greater than myself could restore me to peace of mind, and it has meant choosing to turn my will and my life over to the care of God as I understand him.

Yet how am I to understand God? As I ponder "a reality greater than myself," an "I am" greater than I am, I think of Jesus saying "the Father is greater than I" even while saying "I and the Father are one,"[50] and it occurs to me that there is a kind of self-consciousness that comes of entering into the consciousness of a reality greater than myself. If I am aware of Someone or Something encompassing me, I become aware of myself in a new way. No doubt, this Someone or Something could remain a kind of undifferentiated presence, as Being does for Heidegger. If it does become distinct, though, as it has for me in the encounter with Jesus and with the God of Jesus, it calls forth in me a new presence to myself, the heightened and deepened presence of mind I have been talking about, a consciousness that "it is no longer I who live, but Christ who lives in me."

I had always taken self-consciousness to be my point of departure and also my point of arrival in thinking, passing over from myself to others, however distant in place and time, as in this pilgrimage to Jerusalem, and then coming back again to myself with the new insight I had gained. To take the consciousness of a reality greater than myself as my point of departure and of arrival has called for a conversion of mind, though a subtle one since "greater than myself" still involves "myself." It has called for a starting point like that of Augustine in his *Confessions*, the heart's desire for God, "our heart is unquiet until it rest in thee."[51] From now on, I have resolved, I will start out from heart's desire, though now it seems to me I have been doing this all along, and I will move towards its realization in "Jesu, joy of man's desiring."[52] The difficulty in doing this, I can see, is that we usually suppose, and I usually suppose too when at unawares, that our heart's desire is to be found in some kind of settled happiness, or we do so until our life proves to be about something else, a joy compatible with sorrow.

Our life proves to be about such a joy, the joy of our desiring, it seems to me now, as we come to present mind, to presence to ourselves, to presence of mind that is also presence of God. I came to *present mind* in the Sinai when I saw the Bedouin living in the present and felt the contrast between that and living in the past and the future. I came to *presence to myself* in Jerusalem when I felt left to myself in order for God to know all that was in my heart. And I came to *presence of mind* that was also *presence of God* in Galilee when I felt drawn to follow Jesus, to follow joy, to follow "Jesu, joy of man's desiring." I can see now how present mind without presence to myself is not possible for me, living in the present and simply forgetting the past and the future, and I can see too how presence of mind without presence of God is not possible for me either, living in loneliness without the taste of joy.

To take my heart's desire as my new starting point is to start from a present mind that is also a presence to myself, a present mind because it means being in touch rather than out of touch with my heart, a presence to myself because my heart's desire is the longing in my loneliness, something that comes to light in "the test of loneliness" when I am left to myself. To take heart's desire as my point of departure in passing over to others is really to start from myself still but from a deeper center in myself, a center that corresponds to the center in every other person, as in Hammarskjold's words, "We all have within us a center of stillness surrounded by silence."[53] To come back then to heart's desire as a point of arrival is to come back to a presence of mind that is also a presence of God, a presence of mind because "a center of stillness" means a calm and collected and self-possessed mind, a presence of God because my center is "surrounded by silence" in which God can speak. It is what comes to me then in the silence, when heart speaks to heart, that is "the bread of the Coming One," that is the "joy of man's desiring."

As I left Jerusalem for Athens on my way home, I realized my pilgrimage had taken me from Athens to Jerusalem, from a world where mind has the primacy to a world where mind is a window on heart and soul. God is far and near in thinking, God as the unknown, but God becomes far and near in longing when I seek not only to know but also to be known, when I realize knowing comes of being known. "I think, therefore I am" is overshadowed then by an "I am" greater than I am. As I traveled among the Greek islands, I found myself looking for some symbol of this new consciousness. How do I know "I am"? I was looking for a pilgrim sign, and on one of the islands, Hydra I think, I got a brass cross to be worn on a leather strap around my neck. It did not say "I am" so much as "I will die," and yet it seemed to say, as in the Gospel verse, "When you have lifted up the Son of Man, then you will know I am."[54]

2

A Pilgrimage of the Heart

Follow the heart's desire! That was the motto of my second pilgrimage to Jerusalem. "Follow it," I told myself, "and then you will know the joy of man's desiring." But I discovered in trying to follow it how unfulfilled a longing it can be, how it can seem even an unrequited love. One day as I was waiting with three others at a station in Haifa, looking for the train to Jerusalem, I turned and saw behind us a single small figure in a wide empty space, a little boy calling out "Abba . . . ? Abba . . . ?"

I thought again of the little girl I had seen on my first pilgrimage, pinching her father's cheek and saying "Abba, Abba, Abba, Abba." There was a contrast between that scene and this, between the little girl in her father's arms and the little boy all by himself, between the cry of one beloved and the cry of one forlorn. Yet the cry was one and the same, "Abba." An unrequited longing can be restless, I thought to myself, and it can be peaceful, restless in the absence and peaceful in the presence of the one who loves and is loved. Yet something happens when it is expressed, when it is uttered in a cry. There is a release, and even restless longing is on its way to being peaceful, as when a child cries itself to sleep. So too when I am troubled and heartsore, I pray, appeal, cry out to God until I am at peace. Unrequited longing becomes peaceful when it becomes prayer, when it becomes a cry to God, although I find it still there in my heart, still a longing, still unfulfilled. "Our heart is unquiet," I want to say too, "until it rest in thee," until it is poured out in prayer, not until our prayer is answered, I mean, but until our prayer is uttered.

Is our longing ever requited then, our prayer ever answered? Yes it is, I came to believe during my second time in Jerusalem, during my second colloquy of Jews and Christians and Muslims. I had already come across the passage in the story of T. E. Lawrence where he met an old man in the desert who said "The love is from God and of God and towards God."[1] Meditating on that, I came to believe the longing of the heart is that very love. If it does come from God and go to God, if it is "of God," even God's own love in us, then our longing is its own requital, our prayer its own answer. Then our life is about the love of God. I knew the heart's desire only as longing, however, and not yet as love. So that was my hope on this second journey, to know the heart's desire as love, to know the love that comes from God and goes to God. It was to be more than "a sentimental journey," I hoped, more than a return to beloved times and places. It was to be a quest of love, a pilgrimage of the heart.

"Our heart is unquiet," I learned from experience, as long as we know the heart's desire only as longing. It is unquiet "until it rest in thee," until we know the heart's desire as love, and we cannot know it as love until we are willing, until we hope to "rest in thee." It is as if God were saying "Let me be enough for you" and I were hesitating because what is everything in relationship can seem as nothing in experience. I can say "Yes" only by a conversion of the heart, I found, a turning from experience to relationship, from "I and it," as Martin Buber says, to "I and thou."[2]

The Restlessness of Desire

"How many children do you have?" a Bedouin woman asked me in the Sinai desert. "Many," I said, though I have no children of my own. I was thinking of the many I had taught over the years, children of wisdom, so I think of them, as in the words of Jesus, "Yet wisdom is justified by all her children."[3] They are wisdom's and my children, or so I think. I was surprised, nevertheless, by the woman's question and even more by my own answer. I had not realized how unwilling I am to be childless, how strongly I desire to have children of my own, how I see wisdom in my life "justified," or verified as wisdom, "by all her children." The woman's question was straightforward, it is true. A straightforward answer would have been "None." Yet that was not what she was expecting. She had not asked "Do you have any children?" but "How many children do you have?" No doubt, she was expecting some number like "Three" or "Five" or "Seven." My answer "Many" was a strange one, therefore, and even without explanation may have conveyed some of my meaning. It set me thinking, at any rate, about my heart's desire. Is it for children? Is it for wisdom? Is it for children by wisdom?

There is an ascent of desire, or of longing (Eros), according to Plato, from children to wisdom, seeking always "birth in beauty, whether of body or soul."[4] We start by seeking birth and beauty in the form of children, he says, and we end it by seeking it in the form of wisdom. We seek union with the beautiful, ascending from passion for individual beauty to ecstasy in contemplation of universal and ideal beauty. He speaks too of the "children" of wisdom, the children of the soul, meaning not "mortal children," he says, but the lasting works of wisdom, almost as in the alternate version of the words of Jesus, "Yet wisdom is justified by her deeds."[5] I find my own heart kindled, nevertheless, by the thought rather of human beings as the children of wisdom in my life. That thought seems to unite the whole range of heart's desire, from children to wisdom, in one beloved image of wisdom and all her children.

My answer "Many," I know, can suggest another and opposite train of thought, "the restlessness of desire,"[6] the ceaseless movement of desire from image to image. Instead of one beloved image of wisdom and all her children there can be an endless succession of images, the many shapes that desire can take. In those very words, "Yet wisdom is justified by all her children" and the alternate "by her deeds," there are several different forms my heart's desire can take, a seeking after wisdom, a striving toward a justification of my life, a longing for children, a yearning to do deeds of lasting significance, and all in all a desiring of eternal life. Do all these things come together into one thing, or do they break down into many different things? That is the question that is ultimately raised by Augustine's point, "Our heart is unquiet until it rest in thee," and Freud's counterpoint, "the restlessness of desire." *Is there any rest, or is desire simply restless?*

If there is rest, if there is Heart's Content, as a town is named on the island of Newfoundland, then it is found, as the naming of the town may suggest, only by crossing the ocean of life.[7] It is found only "in thee." If there is no rest, on the other hand, if desire is simply restless, then at most we do things "to our heart's content," as we say, we do things, that is, to the point of satiety. It is the difference between coming to peace and going to the limits of will and pleasure. During my first stay in the Sinai desert I was seeking peace of mind. During this second I was seeking something more, peace of heart.

I found peace of mind in being willing to live with unfulfilled desire even while hoping nonetheless for its fulfillment. I wanted now to come to a sense of fulfillment, if that were possible, and thus to peace of heart. Yet what is it to cross the ocean of life? As I was talking with the Bedouin woman, I was sitting on the eastern shore of the Sinai Peninsula, looking across the Gulf of Akaba. "When the sage says: 'Go over,' he does not mean that we should cross to some actual place," Franz Kafka says, "which we could do anyhow if the labor were worth it."[8] There is nowhere we can actually go to find peace, I realized, not even here in the Sinai or in Jerusalem or in Galilee, not even across the Gulf of Akaba and on to Mecca. Thus there is a literal truth in "the restlessness of desire." No matter where we go desire will still be restless and will leave us thinking "Life is elsewhere."[9] Is the truth of parables and sayings like "Go over" only then of imagination, of "some fabulous yonder"?

It is reality in parable, according to Kafka, but parable in reality. He illustrates with a parable about parables. "If you only followed the parables," one man said, "you yourselves would become parables and with that rid of all your daily cares." "I bet that is also a parable," another said. "You have won," said the first. "But unfortunately only in parable," said the second. "No, in reality," said the first: "in parable you have lost." So it is also, I think, with "the restlessness of desire." In reality it wins, in being true to life, that is, but in parable it loses, in showing the true depth of life. There is something to that thought of following the parables and becoming a parable and being free of daily cares. It is very close to the sense of fulfillment I was seeking, very close to peace of heart. It means living, nevertheless, with restless desire and with daily cares, learning there is rest and yet desire is also restless, that Augustine's point and Freud's counterpoint are in harmony. Still, I cannot find rest in an image, since desire will always move on to another, but only in a reality, an ultimate reality, "in thee."

To follow the parables, to become a parable, to be free of daily cares, though it is described in image, is to be in touch with reality, with ultimate reality. It is reality in parable. I was reading the Gospel of John every day on this second pilgrimage, and in the Sinai I was reading the Prologue over and over, reciting it as if it were a prayer. When I thought of image and reality then, I thought of the opening, "In the beginning was the Word." For the words of Jesus are sayings and stories, and yet Jesus himself is a reality, the very embodiment of what he is saying and telling, "And the Word became flesh and dwelt among us."[10] If I follow his parables, accordingly, I become a parable as "the Word becomes flesh," my reality and his become one, the Word becomes flesh in me. As it was, I saw myself following insight rather than following parables. To follow the parables, to become a parable myself, to be free of daily cares, would be to go somehow from insight to word.

"My relating to God has been especially in terms of insight, as I have understood it, being led by insight," I wrote in my diary. "Maybe now I am being called to let word come out of insight, or let myself be carried from insight to word in my relationship with God." I thought of my old teacher Bernard Lonergan and his teaching that word comes out of insight but that insight is into image.[11] If he is right, parable comes before and after insight, before as image, after as word. Actually there was an insight I was seeking. I had known the heart's desire only as longing, and I was seeking to know it as love. If I come to know the heart's desire as love, I realized, "I am a word of God," as Ignatius wrote to the Romans, but if I know it only as longing, "I shall again be only a cry."[12] That is what it meant to me to follow the parables and to become a parable myself. As yet I was not a parable of love like the old man Lawrence met in the desert who said "The love is from God and of God and towards God." I was only a parable of longing, the man who was asked "How many children do you have?" and who answered "Many."

To go from insight to word, I was hoping, would be to go also from longing to love. If "the restlessness of desire" is a ceaseless movement from image to image, and if "insight into image" is an understanding of the meaning of an image to the human heart, then word as the expression of insight is an expression of that meaning. Such an expression is already "a lover's discourse," even if we say "that the lover's discourse is today of *an extreme solitude*," that it comes out of an extreme loneliness. For "it has no recourse but to become the site, however exiguous, of an *affirmation.*"[13] Love is thus an affirmation of what is already there in longing. It is the affirmation of the heart's desire. To go from longing to love, I gather, is to go from "an extreme solitude" where I feel only the unceasing movement of longing to "an affirmation" where I come to rest in love. If I can only give expression to my heart's desire, I can love, I can love with all my heart, I can love God.

It is insight into image, to be sure, that brings the ceaseless movement from image to image to a standstill. Or better, it is insight that finds a stability in the movement, a rest in the restlessness. Say I go from person to person, from place to place, from thing to thing, always looking for someone or something to fill my life. When I come to realize what I am doing, I begin to understand these images of persons and places and things. I begin to understand this perpetual motion from one to another. My understanding, my insight into image, as it grows and deepens, begins to stabilize me, like a gyroscope or a balance wheel. I become capable of staying with a person, a place, a thing, even though the person, the place, the thing does not fill my life. I begin to understand how no one could fill my life unless it were someone who is somehow everyone, nothing unless it were something that is somehow everything, no one and nothing but God alone. At the same time I can understand how everyone becomes everyone else, how everything becomes everything else, in image not in reality, as one image dissolves into another in the ceaseless movement of desire, as if the universe were a spinning top:

> For in truth the entire universe is a spinning top, which is called a *dreidel*. Everything moves in a circle: angels change into men and men into angels; the head becomes a foot, and the foot a head. All things in the world are part of this circular motion, reborn and transformed into one another. That which was above is lowered and that which was below is raised up. For in their root all of them are one.[14]

In these words of Rabbi Nahman of Bratslav, though he means them to be a description of the universe, I see the perpetual motion of desire from image to image, one image passing into another, angels into human beings and human beings into angels, high into low and low into high, head into foot and foot into head. A *dreidel* is a top, a four-sided die marked on each side with a Hebrew letter, a toy children play with at the Hanukkah festival. If the universe is indeed a spinning top, as Nahman says, it appears so only in the light of desire, it seems to me, and it is insight into image, into the perpetual transformation of images, to see "in their root all of them are one."

Loving "with all your heart, and with all your soul, and with all your might" is not possible, it seems, without knowing "in their root all of them are one," for otherwise there would always be someone or something left out. I would always feel I was missing out somehow on life. Everything is made of everything else, according to some, and everything has its own structure, according to others, a physicist once told me, speaking of views of the universe. Both views are true of images, it seems to me. One image changes into another, and yet each image has its own structure. Insight into the unity of all images gives the spinning top of my life a kind of gyroscopic stability. It gives my life a direction like a gyrocompass. Insight into the unique structure of each image, on the other hand, enables me to determine where I am at a given moment in my life. My situation is changed each time I come to insight, from "an extreme solitude" to "the site of an affirmation." Realizing the images are images, I am able to affirm one and all, persons and places and things, for I am really affirming the heart's desire, "the Lord is our God, the Lord is one."[15]

Here then is the affirmation I come to, the one in the many and the many in the one. Here is the meaning in the meaning of my answer to the Bedouin woman, "Many." When I said that to her, I was speaking out of my loneliness, out of "an extreme solitude." When I repeat it now to myself, it has more heart in it, is more "an affirmation" of love. "Our relation to our fellow human beings is that of prayer," Kafka says, "our relation to ourselves, that of striving."[16] I think I know what he means. We realize we cannot control what others think or say or do, we can only embrace their mystery, our relation to them is that of prayer, but we believe we have control over ourselves, we do not embrace our own mystery, our relation to ourselves is rather that of striving. Or that is how things are in "an extreme solitude." But if we do embrace our own mystery, I see now, if we pass from striving to prayer in relation to ourselves, we come to "an affirmation" of love. What is more, we come to rest.

When I think of the persons who belong to my life and, among them, those I have taught over the years, the children of wisdom in my life, I realize my relationship with them has been one of prayer, of embracing their mystery. My relationship with myself, however, has been one of striving. It is true, "from prayer we draw the strength for striving," as Kafka goes on to say, and that is what I have been doing all this time. It is possible, though, I see now, to go from striving to prayer even in relationship with ourselves, and thus to go from restlessness to rest. I don't mean we can actually stop the movement of desire from image to image. I mean rather that our relation to it can change. As I see it now, my restlessness is not simply in the unceasing movement but in my relation to the movement, in my striving. The essential thing here is to distinguish between the "things of life" and our "relation to the things."[17] The perpetual movement from image to image corresponds to the perpetual flow of the things, entering a life and passing from the life. Striving is a matter of will, and prayer a matter of willingness, in our relation to the flow.

To embrace the mystery of another person is to say "Peace" to the other, as in the everyday greeting, *shalom* in Hebrew, *salam* in Arabic, to think and say and do what is being expressed in that prayer, the very symbol of what Kafka means when he says "Our relation to our fellow human beings is that of prayer." It is to be willing to be at one with the other, an exercise in humility, in "joining the human race," as it is said. "Humility provides everyone, even the lonely and despairing, with the firmest relation to one's fellow human beings," Kafka says, "a relation too that is instantaneous, though only if the humility is complete and permanent." It is the humility of being fellow human beings before God, and so it leads us directly into the depth of relationship. "It can do this because it is the true language of prayer," he says, "at once worship and firmest union." For the mystery of the other is not in some idiosyncracy but in the other's peace of mind and heart and soul.

To embrace my own mystery, my own peace—to receive the peace I so readily give to others—is more difficult for it means getting through the discontent that lingers "at my heart's core."[18] My striving arises out of my discontent, and my discontent arises out of my heart's longing. My striving, however, is a matter of will while my heart's longing is innate, it seems, independent of my will. My discontent lies somewhere between the two. There is a discontent that is nearer to my striving, a sense of grievance or thwarted aspirations or desires, a sense really of thwarted will, and there is a discontent that is nearer to my heart's longing, simply a restless yearning or aspiration for improvement or perfection, an inquietude of heart, a sense simply of unfulfilled desire. Getting through my discontent, therefore, and coming to peace of heart, means going from striving to prayer in relation to my own yearnings and aspirations, from a will to fulfill them myself to a willingness to let God fulfill them. I cannot be at peace with thwarted will, but I can be at peace with unfulfilled desire, and I can go in peace from longing to love.

It is in going from longing to love that a person's mystery is disclosed. Say one's love is the sea, say one's life is shaped by love of the sea. There is also a longing for the sea when one is far from it, "But deep in the hearts of all my kindred lies the sea-longing, which it is perilous to stir."[19] To go from the longing to the love then, or even only to stir the longing, is to reveal what is deep in one's heart, to disclose one's mystery. It is "perilous to stir" the longing, nevertheless, for once it is stirred there is no peace except in its fulfillment, "No peace shall I have again under beech or under elm." All of this, it seems to me, the love of the sea and the sea-longing, is a parable of the love of God and the longing for God. The mystery is the same in everyone, everything is made of everything else, the longing in everyone is realized in the love of God, and yet the mystery is unique in each person, everything has its own structure, the longing takes its own form in each.

Is it perilous then to stir the longing for God? I think of the words in the Song of Songs, three times repeated, "I adjure you, O daughters of Jerusalem, by the gazelles or the hinds of the field, that you stir not up nor awaken love until it pleases."[20] Here too there is a parable of the love of God and the longing for God. Here the parable is human love, that of man and woman. In each instance the longing for God is stirred by insight into image, by realizing the parable is a parable, that the sea-longing, that human love is a shape taken by the love of God. The unceasing movement of desire from image to image is a shape-shifting, a shape-changing, according to this, a continual metamorphosis of the heart's desire. It is perilous to see through all of this, to realize the heart's desire is for God, for then there is no peace except the peace of the heart that is the gift of God, the peace that comes by going from striving to prayer in relation to ourselves. Do not stir it up, the Song adjures us, "until it please," until the time is ripe, until the heart itself seems to call for God.

"I slept, but my heart was awake,"[21] it is said also in the Song. "I slept," I did not realize my longing was for God, "but my heart was awake," my heart was moving restlessly from one thing to another, from one person to another, looking for God. That seems to describe perfectly "the restlessness of desire." It also describes the verge of insight, the moment when all is

ready for one to come to insight, to realize it is God that one is
seeking. I think such a moment came for me when I was talking
with the Bedouin woman, when she asked about my children,
and I began to realize I had children and many children at that!
I began to see then how all the things I sought in my life, to
have children, to have wisdom, to have everlasting life, came
together in one thing, in love of children, of wisdom, of life, in
love of God. My insight was into the image of wisdom and her
children, "Wisdom doth live with children round her knees."[22]

It is said, "One always learns one's mystery at the price of
one's innocence."[23] There is indeed a loss of innocence about
going from one thing to another, from one person to another,
after one learns the mystery of heart's desire, after one realizes
one's longing is for God. There is still restlessness "at my heart's
core," though, the ongoing movement from image to image,
even after insight into image. That is where I found myself
after my conversation with the Bedouin woman. I had learned
my mystery, come to insight, and yet my heart was still unquiet, still restlessly moving from one to another. It is ironic but
we were celebrating the Sabbath that day when the woman
spoke to me, the day of rest when the words come true, "Our
heart is unquiet until it rest in thee." Jews and Christians and
Muslims, we were following the customs of the Orthodox Jews
that day. I was struck by the way the Sabbath is envisioned as a
feminine figure in Jewish liturgy,[24] a figure like the Shekinah,
the presence of God, or Sophia, the wisdom of God. It seemed
to me the Bedouin woman who approached me was a human
embodiment of the Sabbath, of the Shekinah, of Sophia. My
heart was unquiet, but I had met the peace of God.

The Heart of the World

Once you meet the peace of God, you long to embrace God,
to enter into the peaceable kingdom, to be at one with God.
You feel the delay then, as if it were "a time to refrain from

embracing,"[25] to wait, to be at a distance. That is what I began to feel after our Sabbath in the desert. We came back again to Jerusalem and went on then to Galilee, and I asked myself in my diary, "Am I wasting a lot of time on these trips in the Sinai and in Galilee?" All there was for us in Galilee was a landscape, softer than that of the desert, lovely too around the Sea of Galilee. It was the landscape of the Gospel. I used to rise every morning at dawn and go swimming alone in the Sea of Galilee, a spiritual as well as a physical exercise. "The landscape thinks itself in me,"[26] Cézanne says. So it was for me. The landscape was thinking itself in me, I see now, and the Gospel was thinking itself in me, and my own mystery was thinking itself in me.

"I can turn to my destiny like a bather in the sea at dawn, who has just come down to the shore alone," D. H. Lawrence has his Christ say, "the man who died."[27] I could turn to my destiny too, it seemed to me, as I came each morning alone to swim in the Sea of Galilee, not a destiny apart from the Gospel, a purely personal destiny as Lawrence was envisioning, but a destiny in the light of the Gospel, a fulfillment of the longing for God. "The landscape thinks itself in me," I could have said, for I was filled with the thought of Jesus teaching here and also of him going apart here to pray in a solitary place or on a mountain. I was filled also with the thought of what he was saying to others in his teaching and to God in his praying. I took the Lord's Prayer in Matthew and Luke to be a summary of his teaching as well as his praying, and I took the prayer at the end in John to be an expansion of the Lord's Prayer.[28] I was filled with the thought of my own mystery, my own destiny in these terms, of going from striving to prayer in relation to my own yearnings and disappointments and of letting his prayer become my prayer, his God my God.

Still, there was that feeling of wasting time, also of having no time to myself except that moment of swimming alone at dawn. I was doing nothing, as it seemed, that was it, but doing nothing did not really mean nothing happening. Something was indeed happening in me. If it is true, "The landscape thinks itself in me," it is also true, as Lévi-Strauss says, "myths get thought in man unbeknownst to him" and even, as he goes on to say, "my work gets thought in me unbeknown to me."[29] So it was for me, even though I was doing nothing. Myths were getting thought in me unbeknown to me. When I say "myths," I mean "stories" but with a difference. There is the beginning of a story, the ending of a story, the turning point of a story, but then there is a story of the beginning, a story of the ending, a story of the turning point, and it is these latter I call "myths." In particular, a story of intimacy and of distance was being thought of in me, of God being near at hand and of God being far away. I speak of myth because of the story form it took, but what was thinking itself in me was no less real than the landscape. I was meeting the God of Jesus.

I was meeting a God who is near at hand, for I was thinking thoughts of peace, and the peace of God was being given to me, but a God who is also far away, for I had still to receive the gift, to accept it, to take it into my heart. "One of our contemporaries is cured of his torment simply by contemplating a landscape,"[30] Albert Camus says. It was so and yet not so for me. I was cured of my torment by contemplating the landscape of the Gospel, but I could still feel the longing, the waiting, the distance.

A myth was getting thought in me like that of "the heart of the world," a story told by Rabbi Nahman, that the world has a heart that longs for God with unrequited longing. At one end of the world there is a spring of water, Nahman says, and at the other there is a heart that longs for the spring, and in between there is a lowland that ever separates them from each other:

> Why doesn't the heart go toward the spring if it so longs for it? Because, as soon as it wants to approach the hill, it can no longer see the peak and cannot look at the spring. (When one stands opposite a mountain, one sees the top of the slope of the mountain where the spring is situated, but as soon as one ap-

proaches the mountain, the top of the slope disappears—at least visually—and one cannot see the spring.) And if the heart will no longer look upon the spring, its soul will perish, for it draws all its vitality from the spring. And if the heart would expire, God forbid, the whole world would be annihilated, because the heart has within it the life of everything. And how could the world exist without its heart? And that is why the heart cannot go to the spring but remains facing it and yearns and cries out.[31]

Although the story is told of the heart of the world, it is really, I think, about the human heart, about the distance we feel and the intimacy we long for with God. Insight into image here is like understanding an elegy, a lamentation over death or unrequited love. Only here love and death are the horns of a dilemma. How is it possible to find our way between death and unrequited love? That is the question for insight. Or to put it in terms of God, how to find our way between the presence and the absence of God? For God cannot be wholly absent if the heart "draws all its vitality from the spring."

Here is a clue. If God is the spring of water, and if the heart "draws all its vitality from the spring" simply by looking upon the spring, then looking is already like drinking. It is like being cured of one's torment simply by contemplating a landscape. There is life, there is contemplation, there is contemplative life already in the heart's longing if I follow my heart and its longing, however unrequited. On the other hand, there is a withering of the heart, a dying that comes of losing sight of the spring of water, of losing sight of God. Contemplation then, or the contemplative life, is the answer, is the rest in the restlessness of the heart. I can walk lightly, it seems, if I walk in contemplation of God, drawing all the vitality, all the sustenance I need from the eternal spring of water, resting my mind in the paths of the heart, as in the Psalms, in the mysterious ways of God with human beings.

If I take contemplation thus to be mindfulness of God, keeping God in mind, I do run up against a difficulty, that our attention wavers, that it swerves away from God—again the unceasing movement of desire. There is a way, nevertheless, of bringing desire into the service of contemplation, of letting it become a lifting of the mind and heart to God, and that is by taking the incessant movement from image to image as a rejection of one image after another, "not this, not that" (*neti, neti*) as is said in the Upanishads,[32] "not this image, not that image," letting the movement carry us therefore from image to reality. It is true, desire keeps on moving towards further images. It is insight that goes from image to reality. The insight arises, though, out of the unceasing movement of desire. Contemplation, I gather from this, means going with the movement of desire, even with the movements of the eye, or of the mind's eye, only to come to rest again and again in insight. I think of the three movements of contemplation,[33] the linear from image to image, the oblique from image to insight, and the circular around insight, around understanding.

Losing sight of God, losing sight of the spring of water, would mean going from image to image, from scene to scene in the lowland, without ever coming to insight. It would mean living in a darkness that withers the heart. God is not really an object among other objects, according to this, so much as a light in which objects can be known. Thus in going from object to object I never come upon an object that is God, though I may indeed come to see the light that is God. So to lose sight of God is to be without that light. "God does not die on the day when we cease to believe in a personal deity," Dag Hammarskjold says, "but we die on the day when our lives cease to be illumined by the steady radiance, renewed daily, of a wonder, the source of which is beyond all reason."[34]

Even without ceasing to believe in God we can encounter the darkness, it seemed to me when we were staying down by the Sea of Galilee. It may have been only the feeling that comes on me when I am below sea level, as I thought at the time, the depression of spirit I had felt even more when we stopped by the Dead Sea. I was truly in the lowland. The Jordan river comes out of its sources in the north and flows down into the Sea of Galilee, flowing in at the north and out at the south, then on down into the Dead Sea where it comes to an end. We seemed to be acting out Nahman's story, following the river back and up to its sources, and ending in the headwaters at Banyas, the place that was called Caesarea Philippi in the time of Jesus. It is as if we were the heart of the world trying to reach the spring of water. If "love is a direction," as Simone Weil says, "and not a state of the soul,"[35] our physical journey was the embodiment of a spiritual journey towards God in which all is lost at times but the direction of love, the movement itself towards God, when the heart cannot taste the spring "but remains facing it and yearns and cries out."

My heart rose as we approached the source of the water. I thought of what had happened at this place, at Caesarea Philippi, the naming "Thou art the Christ" and "thou art Peter," and then the rebuking, Peter saying "this shall not be unto thee," Jesus saying "thou savourest not the things that be of God."[36] I too came away with a name and a rebuke. My name too was my life seen in the light of the Gospel ("thou art . . . ") and my rebuke too was not savouring the things of God ("thou savourest not . . . "). For to savour them is indeed to taste of the spring of water, not to savour them is to have feeling only for human consolation and desolation. "O Caesarea Philippi," Dag exclaims, thinking of his own life, "to accept condemnation of the Way as its fulfilment, its definition, to accept this both when it is chosen and when it is realized."[37] To follow the Way, I could see, is to go down into the lowland, as the story warns, but it is to come nonetheless to the spring of water. It is to die and to live.

It is as if the human heart does go to the eternal spring in the passion of Jesus, does pass through a valley of tears where it comes face to face with death and darkness, "My God, my

God, why hast thou forsaken me?" Then something happens in the resurrection of Jesus, in passing through death to life, through darkness to light, through heartbreak to love, that allows the spring to flow in time where otherwise it would flow only in eternity:

> And the spring has no time; it does not exist in time. (The spring has no worldly time, no day or moment, for it is entirely above time.) The only time the spring has is that one day the heart grants it as a gift. . . . As the day is about to come to its end, before it finishes and ceases, the True Man of Kindness comes and gives a gift of a day to the heart. And the heart gives the day to the spring. And again the spring has time.[38]

I was thinking of time on the day before we came to the headwaters of the Jordan. "I have no time to myself in this land," I wrote in my diary, but then, after thinking about that for a while, I added, "I have the Lord of time." On my first pilgrimage I was trying to cope with loss and absence in time, and I came to a sense of presence, of present mind, of presence to myself, of presence of mind that is also presence of God. On this second pilgrimage I was struggling with the restlessness of my own heart, with a kind of perpetual motion in time, the restless movement of desire from image to image, and I was looking for a *point d'appui*, a point of support or of rest, and I thought to find it in insight. To bring eternity into time, I was thinking, is to gain insight into image. Of insight we can say, as of the instant, that "it does not scan the passage of time in linear fashion as the Aristotelian water clock does,"[39] measuring the restless movement of the heart. It is rather the still point in the turning waterwheel, the heart's repose.

As I think further now on the spring flowing in time, I am struck by the thought of time as a gift, that the True Man of Kindness gives time to the heart and the heart gives it to the spring. The time given to the heart is the time of longing, and that given to the spring is the time of flowing. What is more, it is the heart that gives time to the spring. I gather that the time of longing is the time of flowing, the longing is the flowing, our longing for God is God's life flowing in us. Insight here is realizing this, realizing our movement towards God is God's movement in us, realizing a love that is towards God is a love that is from God. What the True Man of Kindness gives then, in giving time to the heart, what Jesus gives in revealing God to us, is insight into the heart's desire. When I say "I have no time to myself," I am feeling the need of this gift of time, and when I say "I have the Lord of time," I am receiving insight into my heart's desire, into my very feeling of lacking time, of never having time enough for my desire. I see how time, the restless movement of desire from image to image, is "a changing image of eternity."[40]

It is true, when Plato says time is "a changing image of eternity" or "a moving image of eternity," he may be thinking only of comparing time and eternity as movement and rest. I am thinking of a changing or moving image like a cinema, a motion picture, where there is a series of images in succession to give the vision of a changing scene, very like the series of images in the movement of desire, one image fading into another. There is a revealing then of someone or something, of persons in situations but ultimately of the eternal in us, of God and our capacity for God. There is rest and arrest, true and false fulfillment of our desire, rest in insight into image, arrest in fascination with images, for instance in fascination with scenes of violence. So too there is true and false eternity, heaven and hell as it were, heaven in rest, hell in arrest. I could see the true eternity in the Sea of Galilee, the false in the Dead Sea, heaven in the longing and the flowing, hell in the withering.

"I have no time to myself," I wrote, fearing the stagnation and the heart's withering that comes of giving no time to the Spirit, but having no time, I see now, can go with the heart's longing and the spring's flowing. It goes with a recurring situation in the Gospel accounts that always ends with Jesus retiring for solitary prayer. It comes after the healing of many sick and diseased, after a circuit through Galilee and the healing of a leper, after the healing of a man with a withered hand that took place on a Sabbath, after the feeding of the five thousand at Bethsaida. It comes always, that is, after a period of restless activity, so restless that Jesus seems no longer to keep even the Sabbath rest. He plunges himself into time, into restless activity, but then he plunges himself into eternity, into continuous prayer. "And in the morning, a great while before day, he rose and went out to a lonely place," and "When evening came, he was there alone," and "all night he continued in prayer to God."[41] What he is doing, it seems, with movement and rest, is undoing arrest, undoing that arrested life that is hell on earth.

"I have the Lord of time," I wrote, thinking of his saying, "The Son of Man is Lord of the Sabbath,"[42] but now as I realize more and more the significance of the Sabbath, I see the import also of his healing people on the Sabbath, why it was so controversial. "My Father is working still," he says in the Gospel of John, "and I am working."[43] The Sabbath rest was because of God's own rest on the seventh day after the six days of creating the world. To heal on the Sabbath is to say God is working still, to say I am doing what God is doing, not resting but still working. It implies the seventh day in the story of creation is prophecy, that we are still in the sixth day when God is creating human beings, that the Sabbath rest is yet to come. That seems to be Augustine's thought at the end of his *Confessions*. He began with the restlessness of the human heart, "Our heart is unquiet until it rest in thee," but he ends with God's rest after finishing the world, when "we may rest in thee on the Sabbath of eternal life."[44]

If time is "a changing image of eternity," I realize, we can rest even in restless activity, even in restless movement like Jesus traveling from place to place in Galilee. The Sabbath itself is a parable; God is ever at work and ever at rest. We can rest in the heart's longing, in the spring's flowing. I was having difficulty feeling this in Galilee, though, with my sense of wasting time and having no time to myself. Time was opaque to me; I could not see through time to eternity. Perhaps to see through clearly is to glimpse the eternal vision that comes in "the Sabbath of eternal life." As it was, my desire seemed not for God so much as for someone or something human, for some human being, I didn't know who, or for some human situation, I didn't know what. It is said "when desire dies out, fear is born," but when desire is diluted, dispersed, going from one thing to another, it is weakened, and fear can be felt, the fear that death is the end, or so I felt it, the fear that there is no eternal life:

> I have a sin of fear, that when I've spun
> My last thread, I shall perish on the shore.[45]

I thought of Kafka and his story of the man who longs to go to the Castle, to enter the Castle, but can never gain access to it, cannot even keep it in sight. I had not realized how close Kafka is to Nahman, how like he is to the heart that "cannot go to the spring but remains facing it and yearns and cries out." There is a deep mystery at work here, I see now, that of the "withdrawal" (*zimzum*)[46] of God that Nahman tells of, the story that God created the world by withdrawing, like the tide ebbing, and that if God returns, like the tide flowing, we and all the world will cease to exist in our own right, will cease, that is, to be separate from God, and God will be all in all. Here too the image I am using, of the tide ebbing and flowing, though it describes the world as a tideland, exposed by low water but overflowed by the incoming tide, is really an image of God being far and God being near to the human heart. I see the tide flowing in the kingdom coming that Jesus speaks of, and pray as I stand on the shore:

But swear by thy self, that at my death thy Son
Shall shine as he shines now and heretofore.

Here is where it makes a difference if I am able to keep my
heart's desire in sight. When the tide of God is ebbing, I can
feel the unrequited longing of the heart, and when the tide is
flowing, I can taste the eternal spring in time. Thus the Son
shines both in the ebb, when God is far, and in the flow, when
God is near. He shines even in the darkness of my heart when
my fear of nothingness causes me to seek desperately for someone or something. For I become aware that my seeking is des-
perate. I become aware of my underlying fear. I realize my
heart's desire is not really the someone or something I thought
but the eternal life I feared was only an illusion. So I ask God to
swear his Son will shine, will not disappear like a mirage when
you approach it more closely, that the water I see reflecting the
Son is really the eternal spring.

And, having done that, thou hast done,
I fear no more.

On our last morning by the Sea of Galilee, I found a
strange stone as I came back to shore from swimming, a flat
stone divided by a ridge. It was a heart, to be sure, but a heart
of stone rather than of flesh. Just the day before we had cele-
brated a liturgy in the hills, at a monastery of the Melkite rite,
and I had been given a prayer to read all about the kindling of
the heart and the illumining of the mind. It was as if the stone
heart were the heart of the world, or maybe my own heart,
already withered from losing sight of the heart's desire, and I
was to pray for a kindling, for an illuminating. As we took the
road to Jerusalem in the evening I thought of the blind man
who called out to Jesus on that road, "have mercy on me," the
prayer since known as "the prayer of the heart."[47] It could be the

prayer of my heart, I thought, even the prayer of the heart of the world.

The Unceasing Prayer of the Heart

I did meet a blind man one day, after we had come to Jerusalem, and I found a clue to the mystery of blindness and seeing. I had taken a bus to a district where I hoped to find Hebrew University. After I got off the bus I saw a young man who was blind and his seeing-eye dog waiting at a crossing where many roads met. The dog was bewildered by the traffic and was hesitant to cross. I said to the young man, "Do you wish to cross to the sidewalk on the other side?" He said "Yes." And so I said, "I will lead you." After we had crossed he asked me, "Where are you going?" I said, "To Hebrew University, though I do not know the way from here." He said, "That is where I am going. I will lead you." So we set out, the dog in the lead, then the blind man, and then me. When we arrived I thanked him, and I realized I had seen a parable enacted. I knew the parable, "if the blind lead the blind, both shall fall into the ditch,"[48] but this was a different parable, I thought, where the seeing lead the blind and the blind lead the seeing.

In the parable of the blind leading the blind I see the groping, the stumbling, the falling into the ditch that occurs when we act on sheer feeling rather than on insight into feeling. In the parable I had come into, where the blind lead the seeing, I can descry something else, a seeing that comes of feeling, a light that comes of a passionate desire for light. "My desire for the truth was one sole prayer,"[49] Edith Stein says, looking back on her life. Her desire was for the truth, not knowing what the truth would be, she seems to be saying, and when she came afterwards to see the truth in God or in a human relationship with God, she realized her desire had been prayer all along, unknowing prayer. So it always is with the heart's longing, I believe now, whether it takes the form of a longing for life, as when we are facing death, or for light, as when we are searching for truth, or for love, as when we are looking for someone or something to fill our heart.

To realize my desiring has been prayer all along is the work of my mind leading my heart, as when I led the blind man, but it is also the work of my heart leading my mind, as when the blind man led me. Left to itself, the heart is blind, stumbling, groping, falling into the ditch, going from one person to another, from one place to another, from one thing to another, looking for life and light and love. The mind is seeing, knowing it is "not this, not that," knowing no person, no place, no thing will ever satisfy the heart. Yet only the heart itself can say what does satisfy the heart, only the heart can sense its own fulfillment, as when Edith Stein read the autobiography of Saint Teresa of Avila and exclaimed, "This is the truth!"[50] Her mind alone could not say that, simply from reading an autobiography, but only her mind prompted by her heart, sensing the kind of relationship with God her heart had unconsciously been seeking. It is by following my heart, by tracing the steps of my heart, that my mind can say my heart's desiring is unknowing prayer. Meanwhile, as I come to realize it is prayer, my unknowing prayer becomes knowing.

It can be painful to go from unknowing to knowing prayer. Yet this is what it means, I believe, for the blind to see. It can be painful, like coming out of the pleasant darkness of a theatre into the intense bright light of the afternoon. The pain comes of being unable any longer to feed on illusion, especially to me the illusion that has been most important, that some one human being is my heart's desire and can indeed fill my heart. As the illusion becomes untenable, I feel the pain of losing it even more than the joy of finding my true heart's desire in God. I am tempted to live in a sadness of disillusionment rather than in a joy of realizing "This is the truth!" Here is the choice I was facing in Jerusalem, my truth or my illusion. Am I willing, I wondered, to be the blind man who sees?

A blind man who sees, I found, is still a blind man. We were staying at En Karam, a village to the west of Jerusalem, from which we could go into the city every day, like blind beggars asking for sight, hoping to see with our hearts. All the while we were talking with each other about prayer, asking each group in turn, Jews and Christians and Muslims, "teach us to pray."[51] I wanted to learn to pray consciously the unconscious prayer of the heart. My heart's longing is still unknowing, I found, even after I know God is my heart's desire. It is still unknowing prayer, still groping and stumbling and falling, though it is on its way to becoming prayer that is knowing. There is a process here, I learned, converse to the one described in *The Way of a Pilgrim* where conscious prayer begins on one's lips, then goes into one's thoughts, and finally into one's heart.[52] Unconscious prayer is in one's heart from the beginning, as the heart's longing for life and light and love, then it goes into one's thoughts, the mind leading the heart and the heart leading the mind, and finally into conscious expression, as prayer on one's lips.

I felt akin to the Russian pilgrim, the narrator of *The Way of a Pilgrim*, who wanted to learn how to "pray without ceasing," and went from one preacher to another, then from one spiritual guide to another, until finally he met a spiritual guide who taught him "the prayer of the heart." I felt akin, except that I was starting at the other end. I had already found something that went on without ceasing in my life, the restless movement of desire, and I had seen that desire is an unconscious yearning for God. What I sought therefore was not so much to pray without ceasing as to make my unceasing desire a conscious prayer. Where the Russian pilgrim went from one spiritual guide to another, I went from one religion to another in our meeting of Jews and Christians and Muslims. Each religion, I thought, had something to teach me about prayer. In fact, as long as we talked of prayer, our conversations were a sharing of light, but when they went from prayer to politics they became heat without light, feeling without seeing.

There is the same heat without light, the same feeling without seeing in the restless movement of desire. It makes me
wonder if in going from prayer to politics we were going from
knowing to unknowing desire, and if in going from politics to
prayer we were going from an unknowing to a knowing relation
to God and to one another. I think again of Kafka's saying,
"Our relation to our fellow human beings is that of prayer, our
relation to ourselves that of striving." Our going from prayer to
politics was indeed a going from prayer to striving, from conversation with one another to conversation with ourselves. I
met a small circle of disciples of Martin Buber in Jerusalem at
this time, and I learned about Buber's own road from a mysti-
cism in which there is "no more Thou in the I," as he said, in
which he could advocate the collective spirit of nationalism and
war, to a complete turnabout in which dialogue, "I and Thou,"
is the relation among human beings and between human beings and God. Our own conversations, it seemed to me, as they
went from prayer to politics and then from politics to prayer,
were going back and forth on "the road to I and Thou."[53]

My own road from unconscious to conscious prayer, I began
to see, has also to be "the road to I and Thou," for it means
going from the "I and it" of the lonely heart hunting for an
object to the "I and thou" of heart speaking to heart. Buber's
road was from experience to relation, from seeking an experience of ecstasy that would carry him out of "the commotion of
our human life"[54] to seeking a relation of person to person, of
person to God, in the very midst of our life and its commotion.
My own road, I could see by comparison, is from the experience of the commotion itself, understood as "the restlessness of
desire," to rest in a relation of person to person, of person to
God. I too must turn from experience to relation, I learned,
from seeking experience, that is, to living in relation, from
seeking love as "a state of soul" to living in love as "a direction,"
if I am to find a peace that pervades the whole of life.

I found in relation, in the "I and thou" with God, the key to prayer in Judaism and Christianity and Islam. As we spoke with one another of prayer, I was speaking of Christian prayer, of the Lord's Prayer and of its expansion in the prayer of Jesus at the Last Supper (John 17), when one of the Jews present said suddenly, "Explain to us the Trinity." "Yes," said one of the Muslims too, "explain to us the Trinity." I stopped, taken by surprise. Then I began to explain, as best I could, in terms of the "I and thou" of the human being with God. "Let me draw a simple diagram," I said, and went over to a blackboard and wrote "human being———God." As I turned to explain, the first questioner said, "That *is* a simple diagram!" Everyone laughed, and I did too, but I said, "There is more," and then I wrote under "God" the name "Abba" and under "human being" the name "Jesus." Then I turned the line between into a double arrow "<———>," and I wrote over it the word "Spirit." Then I erased "Jesus" and wrote "I" and erased "Abba" and wrote "Thou." The Trinity, the Father and the Son and the Holy Spirit, does not appear when we consider God alone, I was saying, but only when we consider the human being in relation to God.

	(Spirit)			(Spirit)	
human being	<———>	God	human being	<———>	God
(Jesus)		(Abba)	(I)		(Thou)

"Only the hand that erases can write the true thing," I said to myself, quoting Meister Eckhart. Then I quoted Eckhart aloud to the others, "When God laughs to the soul, and the soul laughs back to God, the Trinity is born."[55] The laughter is a to-and-fro movement of joy, a fulfillment, as it seems, of the restless movement of desire. It is the to-and-fro of the Holy Spirit, coming from God to us and going from us to God. It is the movement of love "from God and of God and towards God." The erasing, on the other hand, when I erased "Jesus" and wrote "I" and erased "Abba" and wrote "Thou," is our entering into the to-and-fro, our entering into the "I and thou" with God, into the life of the Father and the Son and the Holy Spirit. It is our entering not at any point but at a very definite point, in the place of the Son, so we stand in his relation to the Father, as in his prayer at the Last Supper, "I in them and thou in me."[56]

"Why Jesus?" That was the response of the Jews and the Muslims. "Why not Moses?" "Why not Mohammed?" The "I and thou" with God made sense to them, but not the entering into the place with Jesus. All I could think to say on the spur of the moment was that from a Christian point of view God is on both sides of our relationship with God, on both sides of the "I and thou," that Jesus is "I" in us, and God is "thou" in him. I used "the prayer of the heart" to illustrate, for the prayer begins on your lips, goes into your thoughts, and ends in your heart. It is Christ on your lips, then Christ in your thoughts, and ultimately Christ in your heart, as in the words "that Christ may dwell in your hearts by faith." As I said this, though, I wondered to myself how I might come at all this the other way around, starting from the restless longing of the heart, going through insight into the heart's desire, and ending in unending prayer of the heart, God laughing to the soul and the soul laughing back to God. Is prayer going into the heart and prayer coming out of the heart one and the same, like the laugh going to-and-fro?

Yes, I am convinced that it is. I think again of the words of the Bach cantata, "Jesu, Joy of Man's Desiring." He is the joy of our desiring: Jesus going into the heart and desire coming out of the heart meet in joy. Yet I had no words to interpret this to Jews and Muslims until afterwards when I came across a passage in *I and Thou* where Buber, speaking from a Jewish standpoint, is able to speak of Jesus living in "unconditional relation" with God:

> And to anticipate by taking an illustration from the realm of unconditional relation: how powerful even to being overpower-

ing, and how legitimate, even to being self-evident, is the saying of *I* by Jesus! For it is the *I* of unconditional relation in which the man calls his *Thou* Father in such a way that he himself is simply Son, and nothing else but Son. Whenever he says *I* he can only mean the *I* of the holy primary word that has been raised for him into unconditional being. If separation ever touches him, his solidarity of relation is the greater; he speaks to others only out of this solidarity. It is useless to seek to limit this *I* to a power in itself or this *Thou* to something dwelling in ourselves, and once again to empty the real, the present relation, of reality. *I* and *Thou* abide; every one can say *Thou* and is then *I*, every one can say Father and is then Son: reality abides.[57]

It is true, "unconditional relation" can be abstracted from Jesus, considered without reference to Jesus, and thus "every one can say *Thou* and is then *I*, every one can say Father and is then Son," and so it leaves us with the question "Why Jesus?" If I do not abstract it from Jesus, however, if I do consider it in reference to Jesus, it is still true, I can say *Thou* and am then *I*, can say Father and am then Son, but in saying so I am entering into the place of Jesus, into his relation with God. I think it is a question therefore of image and insight, of insight into image. Here is how I answer the question for myself now. Why Jesus? Because insight is insight into image. Take away the image and you take away the insight. Jesus is the image in which we come to understand what it means to live in "unconditional relation" with God, the image really in which we come to understand the unconditional love of God. Take away Jesus and you take away also the relation with God, you take away unconditional love.

You take away the insight, I mean, not the abstract concept. If "Thoughts without contents are empty," as Kant says, and "intuitions without concepts are blind,"[58] I find myself somewhere between an empty concept of universal love and a blind experience of restless desire moving from image to image. I am seeking to find a resting place in insight. "The universal abstracts from the particular," Bernard Lonergan says, "but the intelligibility, grasped by insight, is immanent in the sensible and, when the sensible datum, image, symbol, is removed, the insight vanishes."[59] The empty concept of universal love abstracts from the particular "I and thou," but unconditional love, discovered by insight into the image of Jesus, is known by entering into his relation with God, where he is "I" and his God is "thou." The blind experience of love is like death, "for love is strong as death, jealousy is cruel as the grave,"[60] but unconditional love, seen by insight in Jesus living and dying and rising from the dead, is a love that is stronger than death, that overcomes the cruelty of the grave, that brings the dead to life.

Yet how do I come to a sense of unconditional love? How am I to come to something more than an empty concept of universal love or a blind experience of love and death? If I start outside and try to work in, from prayer on my lips to prayer in my thoughts to prayer in my heart, I run into the truth of what Kant says, "Thoughts without contents are empty." If I start inside, on the other hand, with the restlessness of my heart, I run into the other half of that truth, "intuitions without concepts are blind." The breakthrough occurs only in the moment of insight, I think now, when my mind and my heart meet one another, like my meeting the blind man in Jerusalem. Then my mind takes the lead, illumining the blind intuitions of my heart, and my heart takes the lead in turn, giving substance to the empty thoughts of my mind. Insight is the substance of thought otherwise empty, the evidence of intuition otherwise blind.

Insight comes of faith, it seems here, the substance of thought otherwise empty comes of "the substance of things hoped for," the evidence of intuition otherwise blind comes of "the evidence of things not seen." It is by believing in unconditional love, I mean, that I come to experience it. Once when I was looking in a dictionary at the derivatives of the word "love," I came across the word "loveless." Without any intention of

being profound, the dictionary simply gave three cross-refer-
ences:

1: UNLOVING   2: UNLOVED   3: UNLOVELY[61]

Instead of looking them up, I got up and walked around for
some time, thinking of the connection, unloving because unloved and unloved because unlovely. Unconditional love, if I
can believe in it, breaks the chain of causation. If I start outside
and try to work in, I go from a practice of loving to a sense of
being loved and ultimately to a sense of being lovely. If I start
inside, I come by faith in unconditional love to a sense of being
lovely and being loved and from there to a sense of being
capable of love and a practice of loving.

I think a moment of insight did occur for me when I met the
blind man, when I saw the parable enacted, the blind and the
seeing, though it was afterwards in our conversations on prayer,
and just now in recollection, that the insight took hold of me. I
was aware, even at the moment, of meeting also the one who
speaks in parables, the one who gives sight to the blind. Yet I
was not meeting what he had already said, about the blind
leading the blind, or what he had already done, restoring sight,
but a new saying and a new showing, the seeing leading the
blind and the blind leading the seeing. Now, as I try to formu-
late the insight, I see it is rest, it is repose in longing that is love,
loving and loved and lovely. There is no rest in the blind experience of longing or in the empty concept of universal love, but
*there is rest in the meeting of mind and heart, when unconscious prayer
becomes conscious, when restless desire proves to be unceasing prayer.*

Here is the secret of unconditional love, of living in "unconditional relation" with God: the blind longing of the heart becomes the seeing love that comes from God and goes to God.
That is the meaning to me of the parable in which I took part.
When I think of the blind leading the blind, I think of the
falling and the following that can be seen in Pieter Bruegel's
painting *The Parable of the Blind* where six blind men are shown,

the first fallen, the second falling, the third about to fall, the others following, and they seem to be saying, "For even if we can't see anything, we can still be seen, very much so!"[62] When I think of the blind leading the seeing, I think rather of the consoling and the guiding that can be seen in Georges Rouault's engraving where a blind man is shown leading one who can see, and the words are inscribed, "The blind has sometimes consoled the seeing."[63] To see and be seen are one to little children, when they try to hide themselves by hiding their eyes, as if not seeing meant not being seen. When we come to discern between seeing and being seen, we can discern also between knowing and being known.

To be led seeing by the blind, accordingly, is to be led by an unknowing heart that becomes known, for even if it can't see anything, it can still be seen, very much so! Say I am meeting with rejection in my life, in friendship and in work. If I can believe nonetheless in unconditional love, I can come to a sense of being known and loved, a sense of being seen by God that Nicholas of Cusa calls "the vision of God."[64] I found myself very surprised by his use of this phrase, something I had associated only with our seeing of God in the life after death. Taking "the vision of God" his way, I can see the possibility of a vision of God during this life, a seeing love of God that comes of being seen, of being known and loved. It is a vision indeed, for it is a sense, an experience of being known and loved, not just the bare fact of being known and loved without knowing it. I know I am known. I love the One who loves me.

My heart is like a blind sheikh, one of the blind who customarily learn the Koran and serve as spiritual guides to others. There is indeed something like "the vision of God" that comes with understanding, as when Taha Husayn, himself a blind sheikh, came after many sleepless nights to understand the words "Truth is the destruction of destruction."[65] Memory leads to understanding and to will, just as being known and being loved leads to knowing and to loving. Learning by heart so that the word of God may dwell in their hearts, if I may compare blind sheikhs and followers of Christ, is not unlike believing in unconditional love so "that Christ may dwell in your hearts by faith." Truth does become for me "the destruction of destruction" in that I am led into the truth of creation, the opposite of destruction, the truth that I am known by God and loved by God. For a Muslim who believes simply in creation, "the destruction of destruction" is the truth simply of creation. For a Jew or a Christian who believes in redemption, it is the process by which we return to the truth of creation. For me, it is the passing of lovelessness to love.

There is a destruction of destruction that occurs in the restless movement of desire from image to image, a movement that dissolves what has been called "the imagination of violence."[66] I thought of violence and the imagination of it in my last days in Jerusalem, staying now no longer at En Karam but on the Via Dolorosa in the Old City. There is a movement from image to image that takes place as one walks the Via Dolorosa, imagining Jesus condemned to death, bearing his cross, falling, meeting his mother, being helped by Simon, having his face wiped by Veronica, falling again, speaking to the women of Jerusalem, falling again, being stripped, nailed to the cross, dying, being taken down, laid in the tomb. Following this way is not the same as following the free movement of desire and fantasy, and yet the scenes do dissolve one into another, and finally all dissolve into that of the empty tomb and into the sense that he is risen from the dead. In the end it is "the destruction of destruction." It is "Truth."

Walking this way, I see now as I walk it in memory, means abandoning all false hopes, giving up the hope of finding someone or something to fill my heart other than God. That is what makes it a Via Dolorosa, a "sorrowful road" for me, a painfully difficult route to purity of heart, to willing one thing, a series of experiences leading me through the many possibilities of my life to the one that is truly mine. "Only one," Hammarskjold says, "which you will never find until you have excluded all those superficial and fleeting possibilities of being and doing with which you toy, out of curiosity or wonder or greed, and which hinder you from casting anchor in the experience of the mystery of life."[67] For me to cast anchor in the mystery of my life is to go with my heart's longing for God, to put my hope in that, to let my heart be "the heart of the world" longing for the eternal spring of water. And if I am right about the heart going to the spring in the passion of Jesus, it is to go with him into the valley where one loses sight of the spring, where one becomes blind, where the heart would wither if the blind did not lead the seeing.

"Yea, though I walk through the valley of the shadow of death," I want to say like the Psalmist, "I will fear no evil: for thou art with me."[68] My journey is not only towards God, that is, but also with God. So even if God is far away, in that I am far from my goal, God is still near, and even if I lose sight of God as my goal, I am not thereby turning away from God, "for thou art with me." That is the meaning of God laughing to the soul and the soul laughing back to God, I conclude, that all is well even when God seems far away. God laughs to my soul from far away and my soul, or rather God in me, laughs back to God, for the laugh is the love that is "from God and of God and towards God," and the love is the longing that carries the heart from image to image in "the valley of the shadow of death." To laugh it is enough to know "thou art with me," to know the longing is the love. The blind longing becomes the seeing love in the laugh of knowing and in the knowledge of laughing.

I am drawn to simplicity, as I abandon the hopes and fears that pull me in different directions, for wisdom seems to be in simplicity, the laugh of knowing and the knowledge of laughing in the joy of desiring. Now it occurs to me that the story with which I began has a surprise ending. I was waiting with others to go to Jerusalem, and I turned and saw behind us a small boy crying "Abba . . . ? Abba . . . ?" Then a woman came out of the waiting room behind him and took him into her arms. He was calling out to his father, but his mother is the one who came to him. We call out to God, it occurs to me now, but it is the Shekinah, the presence of God, that comes to our aid. "The guiding counsel of God seems to me to be simply the divine Presence," Buber says, "communicating itself direct to the pure in heart."[69] I call out to God, "Show me the way!" God answers, "I am with you."

Interlude
Heart and Soul

I am with you! That does not tell me which way to go, and yet it is one thing simply to choose a way and it is another to choose the way in the presence of God, in the light of "I am with you." The right choice springs always from the heart, I have been thinking, really from the meeting of mind and heart that I have been calling "insight," and yet the true way is to love not only "with all your mind" and "with all your heart" but also "with all your soul." It is the soul that resonates with the presence of God.

"'Soul' is quite different from what we call 'heart'", Etty Hillesum says in her diary. "There are plenty of people who have a lot of 'heart' but very little soul."[1] One has soul, I believe she means, to the extent that one is in touch with presence, with mystery. When presence of mind becomes presence of God, I would say, when heart's longing becomes love of God, then mind and heart are in the compass of soul. The realm of soul is the realm of presence, of mystery. It is the realm of the unknown. There are voyages of discovery that take us into the unknown, and there is an overall discovery of the unknown itself, like the discovery of a new world. Or it is like the discovery of a limiting principle, such as the uncertainty principle in physics, that when the motion of a particle is sure its position is unsure, and when its position is sure its motion is unsure.

There is a similar uncertainty about the direction and the whereabouts of a person in life. If "love is a direction and not a state of soul," I can be sure of my direction and yet unsure of my state of soul, and vice-versa I can be sure of my state of soul and yet unsure of my direction.

What is my direction? What is my state of soul? These are questions I ask myself in the interlude between pilgrimages. I find that if I embrace my own uncertainty, the realm of the unknown opens up before me, if I embrace my own "going into the morrow" while being "uncertain of wanting to go there," I come into a state of soul, a direction in time like that of Paul speaking to the Philippians, "this one thing I do, forgetting those things which are behind, and reaching forth into those things which are before, I press toward the mark. . . . "[2] I find help in the mystical theology of "the cloud of unknowing" that comes between one and God and "the cloud of forgetting" that comes between one and everything else.[3] I place "the cloud of forgetting" between me and the past, and I place "the cloud of unknowing" between me and the future, not literally forgetting but letting go, not literally unknowing but dropping all my preconceived notions of God and of my personal fate.

It is by "forgetting" and by "unknowing" that I hope I may enter into "unconditional relation" with God, into the relation of Jesus with God that has so preoccupied me on my pilgrimages to Jerusalem. It is a relation that preoccupies me, and yet it leads me beyond my preconceptions. I want to learn how one goes about "forgetting" and "unknowing." I know I tend to live in "the imagination of the heart,"[4] as it is called in Scripture, and I want to learn to live in the simplicity of the soul.

There is a story by Jean Giono called "The Man Who Planted Trees" or "The Man Who Planted Hope and Grew Happiness." It is the story of a man who was planting trees while others were making war, and it sets out to show that human beings "could be as effectual as God in other realms than that of destruction."[5] There is something of the simplicity of the soul I am seeking in that thought of planting hope and growing happiness. It is also closely linked with the purpose of our conversations of Jews and Christians and Muslims. The word Giono is using, however, is *espérance* or "hopefulness" rather than *espoir* or "hope." It is a kind of hope that already includes happiness. It means being full of hope, full of agreeable expectation, inclined to hope, happily expectant. "You know," he says, "there are also times in life when a person has to rush off in pursuit of hopefulness."[6] Maybe that is what I have been doing on these pilgrimages to Jerusalem, rushing off in pursuit of hopefulness.

It is the soul that can be "as effectual as God in other realms than that of destruction," and it is the soul that can survive even apocalyptic destruction, as Jesus says in a discourse on things to come, "In your patience possess ye your souls."[7] In fact, the patience of the soul, as it brightens into hopefulness, can tell us more of God, I believe, than the destruction that comes to pass, more than the Four Horsemen of the Apocalypse, war and famine and pestilence and death. "Because you have kept my word of patient endurance," it is said in the Apocalypse, "I will keep you from the hour of trial which is coming on the whole world, to try those who dwell upon the earth."[8] If peace of mind is in being willing to live with unfulfilled desire while hoping nonetheless for its fulfilment, and peace of heart is in unfulfilled desire becoming unceasing prayer, peace of soul is in hope becoming hopefulness. It is an orientation, a direction in time, that plants hope and grows happiness. It is "the permanent state or condition of living one's life in hopeful tranquillity."[9] As a direction, it is patience. As a state of soul, it is hopefulness.

There is a darkness of the soul, however, that comes of desire being unfulfilled, a darkness of unknowing and of unloving, and there is a purification of the soul, of which mystics speak, an entering into "the cloud of unknowing, in the which a soul is oned with God," an entering into "the dark night of the soul" that falls "upon the road of the union of love with God."[10] If my mind knows God or desires to know God, and my heart loves

God or desires to love God, my soul is one with God or desires to be one with God. When I ask myself then *What does your soul desire?* I am asking what it means to me to be "oned with God," to enter into "the union of love with God." It is as if my soul had gotten away from me, were lodged say in another person, one who is transfigured in my imagination, and I had become dependent on that person or on that figure, and I have now by patience to take possession of my soul, to be at one with it, with God, coming home to my soul and my soul coming home to me.

I have to take to myself the quality of soul I have invested in the person I have loved and have transfigured, the soul of wisdom, of simplicity, and to divest myself of the quality I have taken from the other in exchange, the soul of timidity, of submission to fate. It is not really a difference between me and the other so much as between me and myself, going from fear to love that "casts out fear."[11] Here is the meaning for me of purgation, of illumination, of union, the three stages on the mystic way. It is a cleansing of heart, a receiving of gifts, a relieving of distress, a strengthening of hope. It is a coming into my own, into my own way to God.

"You do not need to leave your room. Remain sitting at your table and listen. Do not even listen, simply wait. Do not even wait, be quite still and solitary," Kafka says. "The world will freely offer itself to you to be unmasked, it has no choice, it will roll in ecstasy at your feet."[12] These words, the last of his aphorisms, seem to describe very well my interlude between pilgrimages, sitting and listening, waiting, being quite still and solitary. Does my soul come home to me? Does the world freely offer itself to me? Does it roll in ecstasy at my feet like a kitten? I experience only the sitting and listening, the waiting, the being still and solitary. Kafka is speaking here of faith, though, that "The mere fact of our living is inexhaustible in its proof of faith." The objection occurs, "But one simply cannot not live." He answers, "In that very 'simply cannot' lies the insane power of faith; in that very denial it embodies itself." If I sit and listen, if I wait, if I am still and solitary, I have faith, I even pray, for "The greatest prayer is patience."[13] I have the direction in time that is peace. I am waiting only for the state of soul.

There is a faith simply in living and enduring, it seems, and it is the source of strength people find in great disasters, in war and famine and pestilence and death. It comes to light even apart from times of suffering, though, in simply listening and waiting, in being quite still and solitary. Once it has come to light, moreover, as it has also for me, there seems nothing for it but to go on, to continue on the mystic way of purgation, of illumination, of union, very like the common way of purification through suffering, of learning that comes from suffering, of nearness to God in the midst of suffering. As I understand it, nevertheless, the mystic way has to do with love more as a direction than as a state of soul: the purgation is a purifying of the will, as in the formula, "Purity of heart is to will one thing,"[14] and the illumination is a directing of the will by insight, by being enlightened to see that God is the "one thing," and the union is a union of wills, the human will and the will of God.

Still, there is a state of soul, and the direction in time leads to the state of soul, though the state is one of "wandering joy,"[15] as Meister Eckhart calls it, as if there were no direction, or "joy without a cause," as if there were no purgation or illumination or union to cause it. There is indeed a peace, a "joy" that does not come from a turn of events, from a stroke of good fortune, and thus from "a cause," nor simply from an awareness of the passing of time, that all things, including all sad things, must pass away, while God remains ever the same, but it comes rather from a letting go of the past and of the future, a "forgetting" and an "unknowing" that allows God a free hand, that makes one capable of wonder, that changes one into a child to whom all things are new. It is true, this freedom from the past only makes one open to the future. It does not determine the future or decide one's personal destiny. I come here upon the uncertainty inherent in a life, upon the element of "wandering." It is by embracing it, by welcoming the unknown in hope, that I come to live in hopefulness, to live in "wandering joy."

I can be in a situation in which there is no cause for joy, in which there is cause rather to feel sadness, to feel hurt at being forgotten, to feel longing to have someone who is there for me. If I do feel joy in such circumstances, then it is indeed "joy without a cause," but it is also "wandering joy" because it is independent of the circumstances that situate me. Usually emotion arises out of situation, and the only thing that is independent of situation is will or direction. Yet here emotion arises out of will or direction, and not even out of that alone, since will can be there, direction can be there, and joy is not forthcoming. It arises then out of free gift, by the grace of God. "It belongs to God our Lord alone to grant consolation to the soul without any preceding cause for it," according to the classical rules of discernment, "because it belongs to the Creator alone to go in and out of the soul."[16]

Does God really go in and out of the soul, and do "even the lonely and despairing," to use Kafka's words, come to experience "joy without a cause"? Or is it rather the coming and going of energy derived from sexual repression, that appears to be "without a cause" because its cause is hidden? If "desiring energy is contemporaneous with its representation in the human psyche,"[17] the sexual realm here is that of expression of desire in image, while "joy without a cause" is a kindling of the heart and an illumining of the mind that comes to pass in insight into image. So the state of soul, though sexual, is essentially spiritual. It is sexual in the imagery of desire, as in the Song of Songs, but spiritual in the kindling of the heart and the illumining of the mind. What of desire itself then, is it sexual or is it spiritual? It is like the concentric and widening circles made by dropping a stone in a pond of still water. It is sexual at its narrow and spiritual at its wide circumference. It is not a thing, like the stone dropped into the water, or like the first stimulus of desire, but is the ever widening compass of the human being.

What if my desire is not really my own, what if it is essentially imitative, I want what I see others want, I am lonely because I lack what I think others have? What if "the dearest of all our illusions," as Rene Girard says, is "the intimate conviction that our desires are really our own, that they are truly original and spontaneous"?[18] Our desires do become our own, I believe, as we realize they are not our own, as the circles of desire widen to encompass reality, as we move from the realm of image and imitation to that of insight and realization. Say I am drawn to another person so strongly that I have transfigured the other in my imagination, I have lodged my soul in the other. My desire then is not really my own, until I take my soul to myself, until I pass from the beloved image of the other to the insight into image that releases my soul from the other, the realization that the image is an image, that the reality is in God, that "God is my desire."

Those words, "God is my desire," Max Gorky saw in the diary of Leo Tolstoy and wondered what they meant. "An unfinished thought," Tolstoy told him, "I must have wanted to say: God is my desire to know him . . . No, not that . . ."[19] It is an unfinished thought for me in the midst of recovering my soul. All I know of God really is the kindling of my heart and the illumining of my mind, the love that kindles, the light that illumines me as I drop all my notions of God and of myself, all my images, as I realize the images are images, I mean. Then I know something of "God is spirit"[20] in the kindling of my heart and the illumining of my mind in insight. I have a feeling I have something more to learn of it, though, something that is still dark and that has to do with my soul, with the life of my soul that is also the light of my mind and the love of my heart. It is an enlivening of my soul that underlies the kindling of my heart and the illumining of my mind. It is a nourishing that strengthens without satisfying, that leaves me with my desire and thus is close to desire itself, "God is my desire to know him . . ." but is really not the same as desire, "No, not that . . ."

My desire to know is to take reality into myself, and my desire to love is to go out into reality. If knowing and loving were one, if taking reality in and going out into reality were one and the same, the reality would be God. For "God is spirit," in the language of the Gospel of John, "life" and "light" and "love." I can love God with my mind and know God with my heart. As it is, "God is my desire," I am drawn towards the reality where knowing and loving are one, God is the one I desire, but it is not quite true to say "God is my desire to know him . . . " For knowing and loving are not yet one and the same for me. Still, there is a link between knowing and loving, a knowing that is loving, a loving that is knowing. Call it "understanding." And in that link is the life of my soul. "I know. But . . . I don't understand," as Avremel says in *The Trial of God* by Elie Wiesel. "All your life you tried to entertain. To make people laugh," Mendel answers. "To do so you had to learn to know them—not to understand them."[21]

It is so, to make people laugh it is necessary only to know them, not to understand them. "I know. But . . . I don't understand," I have to say too, as long as my desires are not my own, as long as my soul is not my own. In order to understand I have to enter into my lack of understanding, my unknowing and my unloving. I have to go into the cloud of my unknowing, the dark night of my unloving. Then as I realize I have been wanting what I have seen others wanting or having, I come to understand myself, to know what I do want, also to understand others, to know what they do want. I come to understand "God is my desire." After trying to explain those words to Gorky, who also knew but did not understand, Tolstoy "began to laugh." "With God he has very suspicious relations," Gorky wrote, "they sometimes remind me of the relation of 'two bears in one den.'" Indeed when I do understand "God is my desire," I become aware of the fundamental thrust of my life, that it is the love of God, and in that love I find light, as "love is a direction," and in that light I find life, as love becomes also "a state of soul." So I find God with me in my very desiring of God.

I am at close quarters with God, "two bears in one den," God is near, as near as my desiring, and yet God is still far, by the very fact that it is still only desiring. "The thought which beyond others most often and conspicuously gnaws at him is the thought of God," Gorky says of Tolstoy, and yet "At moments it seems, indeed, not to be a thought of God."[22] For me it is the thought of God when I am identifying the life and light and love I am seeking with God; it seems not to be a thought of God when I am simply longing for life and light and love. Here is something very elemental: I know the longing is for God, but the longing itself does not know. I can have the thought of God in my mind, I can set my heart upon God, but I have still to see God in the darkness of my soul. God is already there in the den of my yearnings, I can feel it, and I will come to see God at last, I am hoping, when my eyes become accustomed to the dark.

All I have to go on is a sense of life there in the darkness, a life I have always been able to draw on, a life that becomes light in my mind and love in my heart. In itself it is a kind of sustenance, like manna in the desert, like waybread in the wilderness. "It did not satisfy desire," I could say of it, as is said of the waybread in story. "It fed the will, and it gave strength to endure."[23] It is the source and the resource of that patience in which we possess our souls. It is the source and the resource of the faith that resides in simply living, that people draw on in facing war and famine and pestilence and death. To become conscious of it, as I am doing, is to begin to see God, though consciousness is not the same as perception, and seeing God at work in my life and in the lives of others is not the same as seeing God face to face. Still, it is like seeing in the dark, or if night vision is too much a perception, it is like being aware of the presence of someone or something one cannot see in the dark, a consciousness without perception. What I perceive, if I am perceiving it, or am aware of, if I am only conscious of it, I take to be God.

There is a hint of perception, of going from a dim perception in this life, like night vision, to a clear recognition in the life to come, in the well-known words, "For now we see through a glass darkly; but then face to face."[24] There is a hint rather of consciousness in the words that follow, "now I know in part; but then shall I know even as also I am known." For being known is a matter of consciousness rather than of perception. I am aware of being known. So too the knowing that comes of being known seems to be consciousness. I know from being known, I am aware of God because I am aware of being known and loved. I am aware of God as of one who knows and loves. My vision of God then, starting from being known and loved, is a knowing of what God knows, a loving of what God loves, a perception that arises out of consciousness. My journey, according to this, is from consciousness to perception, starting from a sense of presence, going through a night vision, and ending in a seeing of daylight.

"Whoso setteth out for God reacheth him not," Al-Alawi says, "but whoso leaneth upon him for support is not unaware of him."[25] If I set out for God, if I go directly for a vision of God, I do not reach God, I do not find the perception I am seeking. I have to start instead from a consciousness and let that lead into a perception. For if I lean on God for support, I become aware of God. Leaning here is believing, relying. Support is the feeding of the soul, the kindling of the heart, the illumining of the mind. If I go seeking for a perception of God, I experience only my own seeking, but if I lean on God for support, I find more than just my own believing or relying, I find an awareness of support, a consciousness of presence, of being known and loved, of being sustained and strengthened. Before I lean, I don't know if there is anyone or anything to lean on. After I lean, I am "not unaware" of God. My awareness, nevertheless, depends on my leaning, my experience of God depends on my believing.

I can lean spontaneously, it is true, as people do when they are enduring in the face of suffering and death, but if I lean consciously and deliberately, as I am doing now, I come to realize God has been there all along supporting me. The spontaneous leaning is what Kafka calls "faith," the faith of simply living and enduring. The deliberate leaning is what Kierkegaard calls "faith," the conscious "leap of faith." What then does my soul desire? The support, life and light and love, but also consciousness of the support, conscious life and light and love. It desires ultimately to go from consciousness to perception, or more accurately, to "apperception" or "recognition," *to realize God*. I seek, that is, *to go from being known to knowing, from being loved to loving*, for it is in the knowing and the loving that I come to be at one with the God who knows and loves. All my mind is there in the knowledge, all my heart in the love, all my soul in the realization. As long as I am known but do not know, as long as I am loved but do not love, my soul is not yet my own. It is in knowing and loving that I come to possess my soul.

In the end I can say with Isaiah, "thy memorial name is the desire of our soul."[26] In the beginning it is simply life and light and love, then conscious life and light and love, and only then do we name God and remember God with the prophet's awareness. It is one thing to have an experience, that is, another to be conscious of having it, and still another to name it. When I remember God and name God, I am passing from being known to knowing, from being loved to loving. Or am I? I know, but does my longing know? I love, but does my longing love? Here is the darkness of the soul I have been meeting, the difference between self and soul. My soul knows, I will say, when knowing comes of being known, my soul loves when loving comes of being loved—this is loving "with all your soul."

To know from being known is an intense simplicity, to love from being loved is a simple intensity. It is to live, as I have been seeking, in the simplicity of the soul. It is to plant hope and grow happiness. When I seek to know, but not from being known, to love, but not from being loved, I start from nothing and move towards everything, not that I actually reach everything, "Whoso setteth out for God reacheth him not." When I seek to know from being known, on the other hand, to love from being loved, I start rather from something, life and light and love, and move towards something, conscious life and light and love, or I start from someone, myself known and loved, and move towards someone, God as knowing and loving, "whoso leaneth upon him for support is not unaware of him." My very notion of being changes, from "being" as a noun like "reality," when I seek to take reality into myself by knowing and to go out into reality by loving, to "being" as a participle like "knowing" and "loving," when I seek the knowing that comes of being known, the loving that comes of being loved. I turn from the infinite complexity of everyone and everything I can desire to the infinite simplicity of the One who knows and loves everyone and everything, who knows me and loves me.

I think of my pilgrimages to Jerusalem as I meditate on the words, "Whoso setteth out for God reacheth him not," of loneliness, of restlessness, of God being far away. Yet I think of finding God nonetheless, "but whoso leaneth upon God for support is not unaware of Him," of presence, of unceasing prayer, of God being near at hand. I feel I am ready to set out again for God, to go now on a pilgrimage, to reenact in memory, that is, my final journey to Jerusalem, to go from hope to hopefulness, from melancholy to joy, to learn from my own travels how to live in "wandering joy."

3

A Pilgrimage of the Soul

Abba! That is the cry of the Spirit in the followers of Jesus. It is the cry of the soul seeking to return to its origin, a naming of the unknown out of which we come and into which we go. I had thought of it as an expression of intimacy, but on my last pilgrimage to Jerusalem a young Jewish woman told me, "That depends on what kind of relation you have with your father." Calling God that too, I began to realize, can have many meanings, depending on what kind of relation you have with God.

"God is constant. I'm not," as an artist friend of mine once said when in the midst of doing a series of pieces to represent the Gospel of Luke. That is why the relation with God varies, even though God is one and the same. So it is also from one religion to another, I could see, thinking of our meetings in Jerusalem, our conversations of Jews and Christians and Muslims. God is constant and we are not; the relation varies even though there is one God in three religions. What is more, the relation varies from Jew to Jew, from Christian to Christian, from Muslim to Muslim, and it varies in the life of any one individual from one time to another. "God is constant. I'm not" is something that emerges not only from reading Luke, as my friend was doing, where it is said of God that "all live to him," even the dead, that is, but also from reading Matthew and Mark where it is also said, as in Luke, "he is not God of the dead, but of the living," or from reading John where it is said "God is spirit."[1] God is constant, according to these sayings of Jesus, through all our changes of time and place, even our passing from life to death.

"I'm not" because I do change in these changes of time and place, and I do die in passing from life to death, though "God is constant" means there is something unchanging, or someone unchanging, that runs deeper than all these changes in my life, even deeper than my passing in death. I think of the lines written in the breviary of Saint Teresa of Avila:

Nada te turbe,	Let nothing disturb you,
Nada te espante,	Nothing frighten you,
Todo se pasa,	All is passing,
Dios no se muda,	God does not change,
La paciencia	Patience
Todo lo alcanza;	Attains to all;
Quien a Dios tiene	One who holds to God
Nada le falta:	Lacks nothing:
Solo Dios basta.	God alone is enough.[2]

There is a simplicity in those lines, a simplicity of relation with God, that comes of a long spiritual journey. That is the simplicity I was seeking on my last journey to Jerusalem, one where God does not change, where to have God is to hold to God (as in the Spanish idiom here), and where God, only God, is enough.

There is a place in Jerusalem where the words are inscribed, *Talitha kumi!* They are the Aramaic words Jesus used when he took a little girl by the hand and told her to rise from the dead, "Damsel arise!"[3] They became a kind of motto for me on this last journey. I thought of them as I spoke to the young woman who was Jewish, to one who was an Arab Christian, and to one who was an Arab Muslim. I found it was I, though, who arose. I was telling my soul to arise, as if they were symbols of my soul, but I found it was really my self who was dead or asleep and was being raised to life by my soul. I was learning, as Edith

Stein says, "how one may go about living at the hand of the Lord."[4] I was being raised from melancholy to joy.

The Self Yielding to the Soul

I did feel melancholy when I came to Jerusalem for the third time; it may be simply because I was tired and exhausted from the journey and from all that had gone before; it may be because there seemed little hope of interchange among Jews and Christians and Muslims. I know fear and weariness and sadness go together. Speaking of Hasidic masters and their "struggle against melancholy," Elie Wiesel says, "there is a solution to loneliness—and loneliness is no solution."[5] I had taken those as watchwords for myself just before coming, realizing that loneliness is at the root of fear and weariness and sadness. Yet what is the solution? I wondered. I thought maybe I would find it on this third pilgrimage and that it would be connected with the simplicity of life I was seeking. *Is God personal or impersonal?* If God is personal, an eternal "thou" as in Judaism and Islam, an eternal "I and thou" as in Christianity, and I can enter into relation with God to find life and light and love, then there is a solution to loneliness. If God is impersonal, though, if God is simply the life and light and love I am seeking, then loneliness itself is a solution.

It may be that God is personal to the self and impersonal to the soul, that loneliness is no solution to the self and is a solution to the soul. It may be that loneliness indeed is the self feeling its limits and the soul feeling infinite desire. That saying, "Man proposes, but God disposes,"[6] seems to define the limits of the self. I could feel its truth on my pilgrimages to Jerusalem, and especially on this third one when I seemed to be able to locate man proposing in my self and God disposing in my soul. I was learning the meaning of the lines,

for I,
Except You enthrall me, never shall be free,
Nor ever chaste, except You ravish me.[7]

A young monk had spoken to me of the last line before I came, about never being chaste without being ravished by God. A young Arab Christian spoke to me in Jerusalem of the next to last line, about never being free without being enthralled by God. I began to understand that my own prayer on this last pilgrimage had to be that poem, "Batter my heart . . . " I had to propose that God dispose.

When I considered the poem in its entirety, I felt a fear at what I was being called on to do, the fear one feels in love and in death, the fear of losing the self:

Batter my heart, three-personed God; for You
As yet but knock, breathe, shine, and seek to mend;
That I may rise and stand, o'erthrow me, and bend
Your force to break, blow, burn, and make me new.
I, like an usurped town, to another due,
Labour to admit You, but O, to no end;
Reason, Your viceroy in me, me should defend,
But is captived, and proves weak or untrue.
Yet dearly I love You, and would be loved fain,
But am betrothed unto Your enemy:
Divorce me, untie, or break that knot again;
Take me to You, imprison me, for I,
Except You enthrall me, never shall be free,
Nor ever chaste, except You ravish me.

This has truly been my experience, I realized, that "You as yet but knock, breathe, shine, and seek to mend," and I don't know if I truly want something more violent, and "Yet dearly I love You, and would be loved fain." I have thought, if I can only let go, I will be swept away at last. But I can't simply let go. God has to help me. It is the holding to that will enable me to let go.

To have and to hold, to have God and to hold to God, that is the thing I had to learn from each one of the great religions, *Quien a Dios tiene*. . . . Or is it necessary to let go even of God, letting God be and letting myself be, letting God be personal to the self, as in the poem where there is only "You and I," and letting God be impersonal to the soul, as if the prayer in the poem were answered, as if there were no "You and I" but only life and light and love? Instead of little hope I had great hope now of interchange. I had something to learn from Jews and Christians and Muslims.

"You" in the poem, I noticed, is plural, not singular like "thou," for it addresses the "three-personed God." I wondered, as I waited for our meetings to begin, if "You and I" is an answer to loneliness, if loneliness is overcome when we enter into an eternal communion of persons. If God is not solitary, I was thinking, even a celibate life is not lonely, or need not be lonely. I know it is an "I and thou" with human beings as well as with God that is envisioned in the sentence "there is a solution to loneliness—and loneliness is no solution." As soon as our conversations did start, nevertheless, I found myself speaking of the "I am" sayings of Jesus, as sayings that lead into an eternal "I and thou" into which we can enter. One of the Jews I spoke with quoted a similar saying by Hillel who came just before Jesus, "If I am here, everyone is here; if I am not here, who is here?" This is "an enigmatic saying of Hillel," it is said, "in which he lets God speak."[8] It is like the "I am" sayings of Jesus, if we take them to mean "God is here." Certainly, if Hillel can say the words himself, if I can say them, it is an answer to loneliness.

I think of my wonder at my own existence when I was a child. "I am here," I said to myself, thinking here rather than elsewhere, here rather than nowhere, here rather than everywhere. There is indeed a threefold wonder in this: that *I* am, that I *am*, that *I am*. The wonder, "I am here," is not quite the same as the loneliness, "only I am here." I think of the loneliness

I feel when everyone I know and love is far away. In the saying, "If I am here, everyone is here; if I am not here, who is here?" the wonder seems to answer to the loneliness. I think of the signs saying "You are here" that often are attached to maps in public places. Once I saw one where the map had been torn away and there remained only the sign saying "You are here." I thought to myself it should say

> You are here.
> It is now.
> Do not be afraid.

The wonder is an answer, though, it occurs to me now, only if it is full of the presence of God, only if like Hillel and like Jesus I let God speak when I say "I am."

"If I am not for myself, who will be for me?" Hillel also used to say, according to the Talmud, "And if I am only for myself, what am I? And if not now, when?"[9] It is I who say "I am," I gather from this, and not just God, and yet it is also God who says "I am" and not just I, and it is now that it is said, "am" is in the present tense. I think of the way a child, learning to talk, will say "No" and "mine," how will and self emerge together, and I think of the long spiritual journey one has to travel in a lifetime from "No" and "mine" to "Yes" and "yours." I have first to have a self, that is, before I can surrender it, "If I am not for myself, who will be for me?" There comes a moment, though, to surrender my self, "And if I am only for myself, what am I?" That moment is now, "And if not now, when?"

Self goes with will, it seems, and soul with willingness; self yields to soul as will gives way to willingness. It is important, though, not to yield before the appropriate time, before the "now" when I understand what is at stake, not to yield, I mean, before self has fully emerged, before will has fully emerged. Self and will emerge in the exercise of choice from day to day. Every day is "now." If our journey is from "No" and "mine" in childhood to "Yes" and "yours" in maturity, however, there comes a day, as Cavafy says in a poem, when we are called on to say "the great Yes" or else to say "the great No."[10] That is the choice of self and soul, of will and willingness. It is the great "now," the moment to say "For all that has been — Thanks! To all that shall be — Yes!" It is important not to yield before that moment, for if self is not yet fully emerged, it is liable to yield to the self of another rather than to one's own soul, and if will is not yet fully emerged, it is liable to yield to the will of another rather than to one's own willingness. As it is, while "No" and "mine" in childhood is said to others, "Yes" and "yours" in maturity is said to God.

Can "Yes" and yielding go so far as to take away loneliness? Can I say "I am," as if I were a burning bush, as if I were on fire but were not consumed? That seems to be the essential thing here, a self that is on fire with the presence of God but is not consumed by the presence so that only God remains. After hearing the sayings of Hillel, I wondered again about Jesus saying "I am" and saying also "I am not alone." I was thinking of the Gospel of John. Can anyone, I wondered, say "I am"? Can I say it? I thought of the blind man who received his sight, according to John. "Is not this he that sat and begged?" it was asked. "I am" said the blind man. So it is possible then, according to John, for one who confesses Jesus to say "I am" just as it is possible for one who denies him, like Peter, to say "I am not."[11] I too can acknowledge Jesus like the blind man, "Lord, I believe." I too then can say "I am."

Can I say also "I am not alone"? Can I say "I am not alone, but I and the Father that sent me" or "I and he who sent me," as Jesus says in the Gospel of John, or "the Father hath not left me alone" or "I am not alone, because the Father is with me"?[12] Here too there is a traditional phrase, to be found in Jewish liturgy, "I and he."[13] But I feel I am getting caught up in words here. What if I could say "I am not alone"? Would I feel any less lonely? As it is, I do feel lonely and I do feel the presence of God. I could also feel the power of words in Jerusalem, though, as if all other powers were subdued there. It is the reverence for the sacred book that causes this, the reverence of Jews for the Torah, for the Talmud, of Muslims for the Koran. I found myself, as on my other pilgrimages, carrying around a New Testament in my pocket, as if to find in the Gospels the Christian equivalent. Yet the real counterpart, it occurred to me, is the word made flesh in Jesus. And what word is made flesh, I thought to myself, if not "I am"? And if I say that word myself what does it mean if not "I and he" or "I am not alone"?

If I feel the presence of God and yet feel lonely, it may be because the bush is on fire but is not consumed, my self is on fire with the presence of God but is not consumed by it. My loneliness, then, is simply my sense of self. It is there when I say "I am" along with the presence of God. "I am I," *Ich bin Ich*,[14] as Fichte and Hegel wanted to say, is not proper to say, it seems to me, does not sound right, as if I were only myself, as if there were only loneliness and no presence, but rather "I am," both the loneliness and the presence. If I take only my loneliness to be real, I get into desolation where I become liable to spite and to despair and to fear. If I take only God's presence to be real, on the other hand, I tend to deny my own need, to act as if it were already fulfilled. Those words, "I and he," when they are chanted in the Jewish Hoshana prayers, put human loneliness and divine presence back together again, it seems, *ani vaho hoshia na*, "I and he, save now, we pray."[15]

When I pray "Batter my heart, three-personed God . . . " I am praying in this same manner, it seemed to me, for I am entering into "I am not alone," into "I and he who sent me." I am not really asking that my self be consumed but only that it be set on fire with the presence of God. I take my loneliness with me into the communion of Son and Father, of "I and thou," my loneliness that is the place where the Holy Spirit can touch me, that draws me into God but prevents me from being lost in God. "If you are lonely enough," Robert Penn Warren says, "you will never know lonesomeness."[16] He is thinking of childhood, how you feel the wonder of existence and how it is a lonely feeling, you are longing for something, and yet not a lonesome feeling, you are not longing for other people. If you are deep enough in the wonder of the universe, he is saying, you will not feel the lack of human company. If you are deep enough in God, you might say too, you will not be longing for other people. For you find a happy aloneness there, where loneliness is conjoined with presence. You cannot feel the loneliness without feeling the wonder.

I have to admit I do feel lonesome, though, as well as lonely. My loneliness for God seems inseparable from my lonesomeness for human beings. My answer may be in those words of Hillel, "If I am here, everyone is here," where I am God is, where God is everyone is, you are not deep in God without being deep in everyone. "Go deep in your own religion," a Sufi sheikh once told me. My question, though, is my inescapable selfhood, the sense of "I" that seems to stand between me and God, between me and everyone. "Betwixt me and thee there lingers an 'it is I' that torments me," Al-Hallaj says in prayer. "Ah, of thy grace, take this 'I' from between us!"[17] There is a longing for unity in my loneliness for God, in my lonesomeness for human beings. It is what Al-Hallaj calls "the essential desire."[18] My loneliness sets me apart from God and yet draws me into the unity of God. My answer may be in my question, in being lonely enough, in being lonesome enough, to be touched by love.

"Go deep in your own religion." I had heard those words from a Sufi sheikh on my second pilgrimage to Jerusalem, but they came back to me now on my third. I had gone then with two young Jewish friends to see the sheikh at night on the Mount of Olives. "This is a holy night," he had said. I remembered him on a night during my third pilgrimage, when again I went with two young Jewish friends, not the same ones, to a Yeshiva in the Old City, to hear them and their teacher speaking about the Sabbath. "This too is a holy night," I said to myself. I took the words of the sheikh to heart then, realizing I must go deep in my own religion to find my answer to loneliness. I thought of the Gospel of John. "It is really the Gospel of pure relation,"[19] as Martin Buber says, the Gospel of "I in them and thou in me." By going deep in pure relation, in relation with God and with human beings, I could come to understand the unity of God, to realize it in terms of my own religion where unity does not take away distinction of persons in God, where there is "I and thou" even though "we are one."

God does not actually take the "I" from between us, I came to believe, does not take away my sense of "I," but makes it transparent, changes it from "I am I" to "I am." God does not take away my lonesomeness, I mean, my longing for other human beings, does not take away even my loneliness, my longing for God. Although that formula, "I am I," sounds awkward, it does describe well the modern self closed upon itself, the chronic condition in which we live. When the chronic condition becomes acute, when my loneliness becomes acute and I cry out to God, when my lonesomeness becomes acute and I go from one person to another, desperately seeking, I have come to the moment of self yielding to soul, of will giving way to willingness. If I can yield, if I can give way, then I become able to feel presence. I am still lonely, but I can feel the presence of God. I am still lonesome, but I can feel the presence of others. I have passed over from "I am I" to "I am."

I have "passed over," I say, because I come back again to "I am I," and I have to pass over again and again, when I am lonely and lonesome, until I come to live in the standpoint of "I am." By itself "I am I" gives words to my own inner unity, to "pure apperception"[20] as Kant called it, my presence to myself that enables me to call my experience my own. When I pass over from there to "I am," I am entering into a larger realm of experience where I can feel presences other than my own, the presence of God and that of other human beings. I am passing over from the realm of self to that of soul, where self still exists but no longer in relation only to itself. It is a subtle change when I pass over, but there is such a feeling of truth about it that I think I understand how Al-Hallaj could exclaim, "I am the Truth!" To live in the standpoint of "I am," I have to believe in "I am," to believe in the truth of what I discover in this greater realm. I have to say "Yes" to "the great word that is very slowly spoken by the shining of the stars."[21] I have to say "Yes" to the word made flesh.

Is the word made flesh in Jesus only, or is it made flesh in us all? That is the question that arose in our conversation of Jews and Christians and Muslims. Or it is the question that arose in my own mind when I compared Jesus saying "I am" with Hillel saying "If I am here, everyone is here . . . " and with Al-Hallaj saying "I am the Truth!" It becomes flesh in us, I want to say, in our response to the word made flesh in Jesus. Here again I am thinking of the Gospel of John, "the Gospel of pure relation," and of our relation there with Jesus, "I in them," and of his relation with God, "and thou in me." I know I come to say "I am" with the feeling of God's presence to us and of our presence to one another only by passing over to Jesus, only by dwelling in his indwelling in us, by dwelling in God's indwelling in him. Then I come back again to myself, to "I am I," and I realize I have not taken with me the secret of "I am." I participate in it, I live in my soul, only by passing over.

Yet what of Hillel and what of Al-Hallaj? What is the secret of "I am"? It is presence that is nearer to us than we are to ourselves, more elementary than "I am I." I come upon it within me when I pass over to Jesus, and so it is something I can say, something Hillel can say, something Al-Hallaj can say. Let me compare passing over to a transformation of coordinates of space and time in the theory of relativity. Space and time for Newton were the "sensorium of God," the dimensions of God's perception of the universe. For Kant they were the human sensorium, the dimensions of our perception. For Einstein it was possible to pass from the space and time of one human observer to that of another.[22] So too for me it is possible to pass over from the subjectivity of one person to that of another and then come back again with new insight to one's own. What comes to light, though, in passing over? For me it is something divine after all, if not the sensorium then the presence of God, the great "I am" of the burning bush and of the Gospel of John. It comes to light in human intersubjectivity, in "I and thou."

Even for Jesus "I am," as he says it, comes to light not in relation to himself, in "I am I," but in relation to his disciples and to God, in "I in them and thou in me." As for Hillel, "I am here" is inseparable from "everyone is here." And when he speaks of "here" he goes on to say, "To the place that I love, there my feet lead me," and to put coming here in terms of "I and thou," "if thou wilt come into my house, I will come into thy house; if thou will not come to my house, I will not come to thy house."[23] As for Al-Hallaj, "I am the Truth!" is spelled out in the verses,

> I am He whom I love, and He whom I love is I,
> We are two spirits dwelling in one body.
> If thou seest me, thou seest Him,
> And if thou seest Him, thou seest us both.[24]

It is spelled out, that is, in terms of "I and he" and "I and thou." As for me, if I say "I am" I want to say "it is no longer I who live, but Christ who lives in me."

If I am lonely enough for God, if I am lonesome enough for human beings, I gathered from all this, I am able to be caught up in a life larger than life, a life that is already coursing through us all. I am caught up in it by passing over again and again to others, as we were all doing in these meetings of Jews and Christians and Muslims, by passing over to Jesus, to Hillel, to Al-Hallaj, but also by passing over to one another. What then is unique about Jesus? The relation itself, I thought, "I in them and thou in me." I come to live in that relation when I let

"I in them" touch my lonesomeness, "thou in me" my loneliness. As it happened, I was called on at this point to lead a little pilgrimage into Galilee. It seemed a chance to let indwelling touch me where I am most alone, to go the rest of the way on "the road to I and thou."

The Silence of the Lord

As we left Jerusalem, words seemed to lose the power they had there, the power to subdue all other powers, and we came into a land of silence, where Jesus had spoken in parables, where what is unsaid is more than what is said. I was given an icon in Nazareth, a nun in the Melkite monastery there had copied for me the well-known icon of the Trinity by Andrei Rublev,[25] and it became for me a symbol of this pilgrimage of the soul. It was the image that went with the poem I was given in Jerusalem addressed to the "three-personed God," if I may say the poem too was given to me. There is a silence about the icon, however, no words over the figures to name them. Instead three anonymous figures are shown seated around a table on which there is a cup with something to eat. The central figure is uppermost in the perspective and looks towards the figure on the left who looks in turn towards the figure on the right who looks downward. In all their faces, especially in that of the last, there is a look of ineffable peace. What is more, the table is open to the viewer, the fourth place empty, as if the viewer were invited to join them.

It is called "The Old Testament Trinity," for it is meant to show the three figures Abraham saw when the Lord appeared to him by the oaks of Mamre. I thought again of Meister Eckhart's saying, "When God laughs to the soul, and the soul laughs back to God, the Trinity is born." For Sarah laughed to herself on this occasion when she heard them speaking of her, saying she would bear a child in her old age. "I did not laugh," she protested. "No," the Lord answered, "but you did laugh." I saw no hint of laughter in the icon, merely peace, but then again that may be as in the story, only Sarah laughs, not the three figures. Laughter, nevertheless, is the theme of the story: Abraham had laughed earlier on, Sarah laughed at this moment, and the child when he was born was named Isaac or "laughter."[26] "God has made laughter for me," Sarah said, after the birth, "everyone who hears will laugh over me." Still, I see only peace as I look from face to face of these three figures here, not even a smile.

"When God laughs to the soul," I thought to myself, means "God has made laughter for me." The laughter of God is the laughter resounding in us. There is in God meanwhile a silence that is full of peace. That is what I was seeing in the three faces of this icon. I thought of the phrase William Vaughn Moody uses, "into the gaze and silence of the Lord."[27] That seemed to describe our journey into Galilee, among the haunts of Jesus. There is the gaze of the Lord, as in this icon, though the gaze is not directed into our eyes, and there is the silence of the Lord, though it is a silence that is full of peace. The gaze is not broken by a smile, nor the silence by laughter. Yet the peace can bring a smile to our faces, can bring a laugh to our lips at the thought of birth in the midst of aging and death. Eve and Cain, in Moody's unfinished play, are walking uninvited "into the gaze and silence of the Lord," hoping to make their way back into the garden of paradise. Yet we are invited, it seemed to me as I contemplated the icon, just as Abraham invited the three, we are invited to sit at the Lord's table.

It is a friendly gaze, a friendly silence, according to the icon, though we have to meet the gaze, to meet with the silence, in order to enter into the peace. That is what we were doing in Galilee, I can see now, and that is where the meaning of the sayings and the parables of Jesus is hidden, in the gaze of the Lord, in the silence of the Lord. As I contemplate the icon before me now, I follow the gaze from one person to another and on down into the world, and I realize that to reenact our journey I have to go backwards from the world into the gaze, into the silence, into the peace.

Our journey into the presence of the Lord took the form simply of traveling around the Sea of Galilee, and visiting the sites where Jesus used to teach. Yet I had the feeling of entering into a gaze that passes through the world, the loving gaze with which God regards the children of God. The Sea of Galilee "had the look," as T. S. Eliot might say, of a seascape that is "looked at,"[28] and we had only to look at it that way to share ourselves in that gaze. As we traveled around it, we came to stand in the places where Jesus stood, as if entering into his relation with God and with the Spirit. It was by standing in his immediacy with God that we stood also in the gaze of God. Only in that gaze, it seemed to me, do all the things he was saying in the Sermon on the Mount come true, about the poor, the hungry, the sorrowful, the outcast being blessed. We stood already in that gaze, no doubt, but we were coming to stand in it consciously, to see and therefore consciously to be seen.

To see, I mean, as in his words, "Consider the lilies of the field, how they grow . . . " It is to see with the gaze of God, to see God's care for all things, and to let oneself be held in that same gaze, to let oneself be surrounded with that same care. There is another sort of gaze he speaks of too in the Sermon on the Mount, that of a man who looks upon a woman with lust, that of an "evil eye" that looks upon another with envy, and that of an accusing eye that sees the "mote" in the eye of another without noticing the "beam" obstructing its own vision. It is a gaze in which I want to have the other, or I want to have what the other has, or I don't want the other to have what I have or to have what I don't have. To pass from lust and envy and jealousy to the gaze of God is to become "pure in heart," as he says; it is to "see God." For "if your eye is sound, your whole body will be full of light," he explains, "but if your eye is not sound, your whole body will be full of darkness."[29] Yet how, I wondered as I meditated on his words, does the eye become sound? I found help in some words of Martin Heidegger on "letting be":

> What seems easier than to let a being be just the being that it is? Or does this turn out to be the most difficult of tasks, particularly if such a project — to let a being be as it is — represents the opposite of the indifference that simply turns its back upon the being itself? We must turn towards the being, think about it in regard to its Being, but by such a thinking at the same time let it rest upon itself in its way to be.[30]

Here there is a turning from having to being that allows me to see the being that is. It is not a turning away, he is saying, but a turning towards. My eye is unsound as long as I am oriented to having, as long as I see everyone and everything in terms of having. There is a blind spot in my vision, an indifference to being. When I turn from having to being, my eye becomes sound, I become able to discern the being that is there before me. I turn towards the other person, think about the other in the wonder of the other's existence, let the other rest upon the other's self in the other's way to be. It is like the gaze of God in the story of creation, "And God saw that it was good." Letting be is creative, is like God saying "Let there be light," and seeing is like the consequence, "And God saw that the light was good."[31] It is like the ultimate consequence, seeing everyone and everything in that light, "and behold, it was very good."

What becomes of having, though, and of my desire to have? As I understand it, having and the desire to have belong to the standpoint of the self. I leave them behind when I pass over from there to the standpoint of another person. It is then that I go over from having to being. I come upon having once more, however, when I come back again from the other to myself. "To have and to hold" then has an abiding significance for me. When I pass over, I go from care for others as belonging to me to care for them as belonging to themselves, but when I come back to myself, I come back to them as belonging to me. As I continue to pass over, I do indeed go from "No" and "mine" to "Yes" and "yours," but as I continue also to come back again to myself, I come to something like the standpoint of Jesus in the Gospel of John, "all mine are thine, and thine are mine."[32]

As we entered into the gaze, it seemed to me, we entered also into the silence of the Lord. I thought of the silence of which Michael Polanyi speaks, "we can know more than we can tell."[33] Passing over, we were entering into a standpoint like that of Matthew and Mark and Luke where Jesus is speaking of the kingdom. Coming back, we were coming to a standpoint in ourselves like that of John where Jesus is speaking of himself. We pass over to Matthew and Mark and Luke where heaven and earth will pass away but his words will remain, and we come back to John where he himself is the word. There is a silence here, the silence underlying the words, what is unsaid in the sayings, untold in the stories, the silence that becomes articulate in the word made flesh. It is a silence that is broken only by the words, "I am," first words, as it were, and by those spoken at the Last Supper, last words, "This is my body which is for you," or as David Daube translates, "This is me who am for you."[34]

Passing over to Jesus, as we walked along the Sea of Galilee, meditating on his message, that the kingdom is come, I kept asking myself the question Leonardo da Vinci used to ask in his notebooks, "Tell me if anything has ever been accomplished."[35] Coming back to myself, however, and to the prayer of Jesus that is also my prayer, "Thy kingdom come," I began to realize that the silence with which the question is met is essential if "we can know more than we can tell." If I ask what has been accomplished, the only answer is "I am." The only answer is "This is me who am for you." For the kingdom is a kingdom of persons, of the One dwelling in Christ and of Christ dwelling in the Many. Take away Christ and the connection dissolves. It is a kingdom of relations. It depends on the resurrection, on Jesus being alive and living with us. There is no resurrection, it seemed to me, where there is no passing over, where there is no coming back. I find the resurrection, I meet the Jesus who says "I will go before you into Galilee," only if I do pass over to him, only if I do come back to myself and find him living in me.

To come back to him living in me and not just to "I am I," I found, I have to pass over to him again and again, I have to meditate on the mysteries of his life and enter into them more and more, like Leonardo painting, seeing with "light-bearing eyes."[36] He is not merely an object, a mangled body on the wheel of the world, but a subject, "I am." To pass over is to go from the object, "This is me," to the subject, "who am for you," as if to answer Hillel's question, "If I am not for myself, who is for me?" "He paid the price for our souls, but our hearts could only be won," a friend has written to me. "He was winning hearts from beginning to end." He is "The King of Hearts." To pass over fully to him, I see now, is to let him win my heart, as my friend writes, "Let Jesus win your heart!"

It is as if the soul were already with him, "He paid the price for our souls," but the self has to be won over, "our hearts could only be won." Heart has to join soul. I have to enter into the silence of my soul which is also the silence of God. It is the silence, that is, of God to me. The soul is already with him, I mean, in the deep loneliness that seems to be part of the human condition, in the longing in that loneliness for life and light and love, but the self has to be won over, to recognize in him the life and light and love I am seeking. There is a silence here because all I have is my own loneliness, my own longing, and the simple words "I am," the words "This is me who am for you," to give it a name. Say I read every night from Matthew or Mark or Luke, as I was doing in Galilee, or from John, as I am doing now, letting that recognition gradually dawn on me, letting the words articulate my heart's desire. What I am doing is letting the poem I was given come true, letting my heart be battered, letting myself be overthrown and made new, divorced, untied, and taken to God, imprisoned, enthralled, and ravished by God, letting my heart be won.

All these violent images are transitional, it seems, on the way to peace, like the ineffable peace in the faces of Rublev's icon. By sharing in their gaze, by entering into their silence, I come to live in their peace. I think of the violent images in black and white in the film *Andrei Rublev* by Andrei Tarkovsky,[37] showing the violence of his times but leading into the peaceful images in color at the end, where we are left contemplating the icon of the Trinity and finally a scene of white horses playing in the rain. We seemed to be going through a similar transition in Galilee, from the violence of our own times to peace, from black and white to color, as we contemplated the mysteries of the life of Jesus, as we let them call forth in us a heart's response. I seem to be going through it even now as I call it all to mind again, as I continue to meditate on the Gospel of John and interpret in its light the three figures I see before me now in the icon and follow their gaze from Son to Father to Spirit to earth.

Meditating on the Gospel like this "dissolves life into the eternal," it has been said in criticism, in fact "all faith dissolves life into the eternal."[38] It seems to me it dissolves violence rather into peace. Violence comes of spirit against spirit, according to the classical rules of discernment, when the human spirit is moved against its own inclination. When I have feeling only for having and I am being carried into the larger realm of being, I feel violence, as if my heart were being battered. Maybe this is a clue to the violence of our times, that we recognize no power greater than ourselves and yet much of life goes against the autonomy of self, of will. Yielding to the spirit that carries me beyond myself, I am yielding really to my own soul, to my own deepest inclination. So there is peace after all, there is silence, that comes of spirit in accord with spirit, of self in accord with soul, "for when it is contrary to them they enter with perceptible commotion and disturbance," it is said of our spirit and its movements, "but when it is similar to them, they enter in silence, as into their own house, through the open doors."[39]

As I follow my own deepest inclination and let it take me from violence to peace, I seem to be following the gaze from Son to Father to Spirit to earth, seeing the eternal in life, in us, more than dissolving life into the eternal. I think again of the words of Jesus in the Gospel of John, "the Son can do nothing of his own accord, but only what he sees the Father doing."[40] Yet what is the Father doing? Working through his Spirit on earth. As I go from spirit against spirit to spirit in accord with spirit, I begin to discern the working of his Spirit. It is like the peace I can see in the face of the last figure in the icon, the one who is looking down into the world. I go from black and white to color as I go from seeing things and situations as they are in the newspapers to seeing them as they are in "the Gospel of pure relation," as I go from us to the eternal in us. Is this what it means to say the Spirit "will convict the world" or "convince the world of sin and righteousness and judgment"?[41]

I go through that convicting or convincing myself as I go from saying "I know who I am" like Don Quixote to asking myself the two great questions of the Gospel of John, "Where do you come from?" and "Where are you going?" If soul is the eternal in us, self comes to partake of eternity by emerging from the imaginary world of desire where I have been living, thinking I know who I am but always moving on restlessly from one person to another, from one thing to another, looking for someone, for something, and entering instead into the true world of desire, as in the prayer, "Lord, show me the path I must follow. Let your Spirit guide me to my true home."[42] Thus "sin" in the Gospel of John is in not believing Jesus comes from God and therefore not believing that we too come from God; "righteousness" is in his returning to God and therefore also in our returning to God; and "judgment" is in his being of God and not of this world and therefore also in our being of God and not of this world. Where do I come from? From God. Where am I going? To God. Or as Hillel says, "To the place that I love, there my feet lead me."

Here the question I posed at the beginning comes to a head, "Is God personal or impersonal?" If I come from Something and go to Something, then I live in "I and it." If I come rather from Someone and go to Someone, then I live in "I and thou." Or I can turn it around, if I live in "I and it," then I come from Something and go to Something, but if I live in "I and thou," then I come from Someone and go to Someone. All we were learning in Galilee seemed to draw us into the "I and thou" of Jesus with God, but I found I could take the "I" there like Don Quixote saying "I know who I am," as he did after his first sally, or "I know that I am enchanted," as he did after his second, or "I was mad, but I am sane now," as he did on his deathbed.[43] My three pilgrimages, it occurs to me now, are like his three sallies, as I go from living in the imagination of my heart to living in the reality of "I and thou." *I come from the unknown, and I go into the unknown, but I can call the unknown "thou."*

When I speak of the unknown here, I am getting away from "I know who I am," from taking image for reality, I am acknowledging the spell of image, "I know that I am enchanted," and I am turning from image to insight into image. "I was mad, but I am sane now." When I say I come from the unknown, and I go into the unknown, I am thinking of the words in the Gospel of John, "The wind [the Spirit] blows where it wills, and you hear the sound of it, but you do not know whence it comes or whither it goes; so it is with every one who is born of the Spirit."[44] And when I say I can call the unknown "thou," I am thinking of the words in the First Epistle of John, "Beloved, we are God's children now; it does not yet appear what we shall be, but we know that when he appears we shall be like him, for we shall see him as he is."[45] For if I say "thou" to the unknown, then "I" will be known only when my "thou" is known, "I" will appear only when my "thou" appears. For the reality of "I and thou" is the reality of relationship, and if "I and thou" is reality, then all is relation, "all real living is meeting."[46] We shall indeed meet in the place where there is no darkness.

There is something terrifying, it is true, about the thought of light without darkness, of life without death, of word without silence. Yet maybe the terror is in the image rather than in the reality of "I and thou." Dread and fascination are feelings that surround images and become absolute only when images are taken for reality. The complete image requires a balance of opposites, light and darkness, life and death, word and silence. Insight into image is a seeing of the way from darkness into light, from death into life, from silence into word. The actual going from darkness into light, however, is not like going from black to white so much as from black and white to color. What I am talking out of here is really "the vision," as Erik Erikson calls it, "of an ultimate meeting,"[47] the vision we can have now, not the vision we will have in the ultimate meeting itself. So I am still in the realm of opposites, talking of a light shining in the dark, a life living on in death, a word being spoken in the silence.

A path can be traced from a primal to an ultimate meeting, from child and mother to human being and God, from looking up into the mother's face, as Erikson says, to looking to the One who will "lift up his countenance upon you and give you peace."[48] Here, he suggests, is the secret of the sense of "I" in the Galilean sayings of Jesus. All the pronouns become important at different points along this path, *I, thou, he, she, it, we, you, they*. Between the "I and thou" of child and mother and that of human being and God there are many relations, but there is an "I and it" that is essential, it seems to me, that of a person's quest of life and light and love, the longing in human loneliness that connects the sense of "I" with the "it" that is life and light and love. Thus in John there are not only "I am" sayings that stand alone, but there are also those with predicates like "I am the way, and the truth, and the life" or "I am the bread of life" or "I am the resurrection and the life."[49] We look up from the one to the other, from the impersonal to the personal God, from life and light and love we are seeking to One in whom we find it.

We look for three things in every human encounter, it is said, even in an ultimate meeting, "the light of the eyes," "the features of the face," and "the sound of the name."[50] This is what we were seeking in Galilee, I believe now, in the haunts of Jesus, the light of his eyes, the features of his face, the sound of our own names called by him, "That which was from the beginning," as John says, "which we have heard, which we have seen with our eyes, which we have looked upon and touched with our hands, concerning the word of life."[51] For this is how we receive and give life and light and love, by seeing and hearing, by being seen and being heard. Is this an answer to loneliness? Yes, there is spirit in sense, knowing and loving in seeing and hearing, being known and being loved in being seen and being heard. What about touching and being touched? That is the ultimate in sense, but even there, I think, we seek knowledge and love. So the ultimate meeting is spirit and spirit, and "God is spirit."

It is in the gaze of the Lord, as I have been calling it, that we find the light of his eyes and the features of his face, and it is in the silence of the Lord that we find the sound of the name, God's name and his, his name and ours, "I am." Here is the secret of my own sense of "I," it seems to me now, the answer to my questions, to go from the "I and it" of my loneliness to the "I and thou" of Jesus with God, to participate in his sense of "I." It is true to say "there is a solution to loneliness — and loneliness is no solution." As I understand it, however, loneliness is in the sense of "I," of being only who I am, only "I am I," and longing for a life that is greater than myself. The solution to loneliness then is the greater life. Or so it is to the soul. It is also the one in whom we find the greater life. Or so it is to the self. The two are together in the sayings of Jesus where there is a predicate, as if he were saying "I am the greater life," but they are together in a more profound way when he says simply "I am." Here self and soul are as close as "I" and "am." They are one, and they are the vehicle of the presence of God.

I know, "God is constant," as my friend said, "I'm not," as if to say "I am and I am not." I am always in the flow of life and light and love, but I am not always caught up in it. In spite of God's presence I am vulnerable to my loneliness. I was thinking of this as we came back from Galilee, when we stopped at Mount Tabor where Jesus was transfigured before his disciples. It occurred to me that the same three disciples who were with him in his moment of glory on the mountain, Peter and James and John, were with him also in his moment of agony in the garden at Gethsemane. There is the moment when the eternal is revealed in us, I saw, and there is the moment when it is hidden, when all seems only human.

All we can do when it is hidden, I thought as we came back to Jerusalem, is call out "Abba Father"[52] like Jesus in the garden. "'Tis Abba Father that we seek,"[53] as Herman Melville says in *Clarel*, his poem about his pilgrimage to the Holy Land. Yet what about the many feelings that surround that name "Abba Father," depending, as the young woman said to me, "on what kind of relation you have with your father"? I thought on that in my last days in Jerusalem and as I went on to Cairo and then to Athens, until I met the curator of the Jewish Museum there in Athens and we had a conversation that turned in the end to Origen and his idea of universal reconciliation. Here, I thought, is the answer. We come from the unknown, and we go into the unknown that we call "thou" and "Abba," but we can hope somehow to find universal reconciliation there, to hear "the word of life" and to speak it to one another, "I am."

Epilogue
The Home of the Spirit

I am! Here is the home of the spirit, where we can hear and say "I am," a kingdom of persons, a life larger than life. When God says "I am," all nature replies "Thou art," according to Christopher Smart,[1] the mad poet of the eighteenth century, but then Jesus says "I am" and we too can say "I am," I have learned, and God says "Thou art," as if to say

> You are,
> You are known
> And you are loved.

We come to this, I think, by passing over to others and coming back again to ourselves, even as we did in Jerusalem, Jews and Christians and Muslims. There is a long journey in which we go from saying like Iago, "I am not what I am," to saying like Paul, "By the grace of God I am what I am."[2] Iago means he is a follower of Othello but is false to Othello; Paul means he is a follower of Christ and is true to Christ. That was the call for me on my pilgrimages to Jerusalem, I see now, to become a true follower of Christ, to come to peace with "I am what I am." I came up against "what I am" on each of my journeys when I came, usually at the end, to a desert monastery. On the first I came to Saint Catherine's in the Sinai and later to Saint George's in Wadi Qilt; on the second I came again to Saint Catherine's and afterwards I went with five Christian Arabs to Mar Saba near the Dead Sea; and on the third, after traveling from Jerusalem to Cairo, I went with a friend to Saint Macarius's in Wadi Natrun in the Egyptian desert. Each time I wondered if the desert monastery is home, or if it is rather a withdrawal that must be followed by a return.

Something happened at Mar Saba that gave me an insight. One of the Arabs I came with was an old man, the grandfather of the friend who invited me. When we arrived, we went out onto a parapet overlooking the Kidron, and after we had supper the old man began to tell a story. It ranged from Damascus to Jerusalem, and by the time the lovers were reunited and the story reached its happy ending it was midnight of Saturday and the monks were ready to begin the liturgy of Sunday, singing into the early morning hours. The old grandfather stayed for the entire liturgy, but the rest of us slipped away to get an hour or two of sleep. I had not slept at all the night before, and so I found it easy to sleep, but when I returned to the liturgy, still going on, I felt something on the back of my neck. When I brought my hand around, I saw blood. I soon realized the bed I had been sleeping on was infested with ticks. I went away and got rid of the ticks as well as I could. Then I came back to the end of the liturgy and breakfast at dawn, coffee and something like baklava. Everyone disappeared then to get some sleep, but sleep was out of the question for me. I remained there in the choir, paging through the liturgical books, reading the prayers. I felt a sleepless consciousness, supremely awake and yet restful. I was exhausted and yet at peace. It is "By the grace of God" if at all, I felt, "I am what I am."

Well, I did not find a home in the desert monastery—I suppose the ticks were too much for me—but I did find an open door into a larger world than that of self. When I am not at peace, when "I am not what I am," I am caught up in my own inner conflict. As soon as I am at peace, though, as soon as "I am what I am, I move into a larger world that exists "by the grace of God." That larger world is the true home of the spirit. It is "the kingdom of ends" that Kant speaks of, except that his, as he says, is "certainly only an ideal,"[3] but this is real, for it depends on the grace of God and not only on our striving to make it real.

Why are we striving? "We go to the Father of Souls, but it is necessary to pass by the dragon."[4] These words of Saint Cyril of Jerusalem are true of every story that has any depth, according to Flannery O'Connor, but they seem to me especially true of the passage from "I am not what I am" to "I am what I am." The dragon is there in "I am not," so much so that the kingdom of "I am" can seem "only an ideal." Our loneliness is real, but peace is real too, I found on my pilgrimages, the peace of being at one with oneself and with others, the peace of being at one with God. The desert monastery for me is a place where one is vulnerable to loneliness, where "it is necessary to pass by the dragon," but vulnerable also to peace, where "We go to the Father of Souls." The struggle with loneliness is the way of passage, the way into life and light and love, but the life that comes of being, the light that comes of being known, the love that comes of being loved is the peace that comes "by the grace of God." Thus *the home of the spirit is the peace of God*, the peace of mind, and of heart, and of soul which is the gift of God.

It is really the story of Jesus that is being told in those words of Cyril, or it is the story of us entering into his story. He goes to the Father, according to the Gospel of John, and he passes by the dragon, opening up the way for us. The question then arises, as the story is retold, Did he really go to the Father? Did he really pass by the dragon? In other words, Is he dead or alive? The answer, it seems to me, depends on passing over to him. As long as he is only an object to me, someone in the third person, "he was," he seems dead. When he becomes a subject to me, someone in the first person, "I am," he seems alive. Passing over means entering into his story, letting it become mine, going with him to the Father, going with him past the dragon. Another version of Cyril's words, this time in the second person, is "Thou art going to the Father of Spirits, but thou art going past that serpent."[5] Putting it that way, I seem to recognize in it my own story, my own passage through loneliness.

When I enter into his story, into his relation with God, I am able to communicate with Jews and Muslims who also stand in a relation with God. As long as he is only an object to me, an object only of veneration, I am in a position that is very foreign to theirs, but when he is a subject, an "I" to me and his God is my "thou," I am in a position to understand them and to be understood by them. I felt this often on my pilgrimages to Jerusalem, when I was explaining the Christian Trinity to Jews and Muslims, saying we stand in the Son's place and that the Spirit goes to and fro between us and the Father. In fact I felt uneasy, especially on my last pilgrimage, when I seemed to find an understanding and even an acceptance of this by Jews and Muslims. I must have falsified Christianity, I thought to myself, if Jews and Muslims are agreeing with me. Then I realized that the agreement was limited. When we enter into his relation with God, Jesus disappears as an object, he disappears, as it were, from in front of us, and that is what they were agreeing with, but he subsists in us as a subject, I was saying, he is alive and lives within us.

It is by passing over to Jesus, I found, that I am able to pass over to Jews and to Muslims, to understand them in their relationship with God. The words of Sufi Sheikh held true each time I was in Jerusalem, "Go deep in your own religion." It was by going deep in my own that I could begin to understand the others. I took "passing over" and "coming back" to be "going deep." For it is a way to peace among Jews and Christians and Muslims, as I came to believe, a way to mutual understanding that leaves each religion intact. We pass over to one another, but we come back again to ourselves. I pass over, I enter into Jewish prayer in the synagogue, into Christian prayer in the desert monastery, into Muslim prayer in the mosque, but I always come back again to prayer in my own heart. I pass over to Jesus the Jew, to Jesus in the Gospels, to Jesus in the Koran, but I always come back again to Jesus living in my heart by faith.

What about the many critical readings of the Gospels in the present age, from Albert Schweitzer for whom Jesus is a "mangled body" on "the wheel of the world" to René Girard for whom he is "the scapegoat," the victim who reveals the innocence of all victims and the violence of human society?[6] All of these readings have in common the viewpoint of Jesus as an object, as someone who is dead. So they can never be more than starting points in a process of passing over to Jesus as a subject, as someone who is alive. The passing over from object to subject is what was going on for me on my first pilgrimage to Jerusalem and my first journey into Galilee. My own starting point, similar to that of the critical readings, was that of someone at a remove of twenty centuries from Jesus, of one who had come to the place in hopes of recapturing the time. What happened then for me was an experience of time dropping away, of centuries dropping away, of becoming contemporary with Christ, as Kierkegaard puts it, or rather of Christ becoming contemporary with me, of passing over to a presence that was then and coming back to a presence that is now, "I am with you always . . ."[7]

All of the various types of figures in history, the citizen, the person, the hero, the victim, come to life when we pass over to them, it is true, but they all become "the dead" to us when we come back again to ourselves, unless we stand in relation to the God of Jesus, who is "not God of the dead, but of the living," unless we ourselves are conscious of being alive to God, "for all live to him."[8] Passing over to Jesus therefore is essentially a matter of entering into relation with his God, the God who is "Abba," who is "of the living," who is "spirit." It means entering into a stance of prayer, that of the Lord's Prayer, the hallowing of the name, the coming of the kingdom, the fulfilling of the will, the giving of the bread, the forgiving of the sins, the guiding and guarding from temptation and evil. Although he is not mentioned in his own prayer, is not there in front of us, still Jesus is there, praying in us, as at the Last Supper in John, "Father, the hour has come . . . "[9]

Going with him to the Father means returning with him to the origin of life and light and love, with him because he is conscious of coming from there and of going there again, "knowing . . . he had come from God and was going to God,"[10] as if he were passing over from there and coming back there instead of passing over, as I always think of it, from self and coming back again to self. Going with him thus means letting God displace my self as point of departure and of arrival. How can this be done? I found a clue in the sense of presence. There is, first of all, "present mind," living in the present like the Bedouin in the desert. I found that was not possible for me without "presence to myself," without being aware in the present of my past and of my future, even if I let go of the past and of the future. Here is where I always come upon self as starting point and end. To get beyond this point I found I had to let "presence of mind" be "presence of God," to let eternity shine through time, to let it be, as if no effort were needed to "practice the presence of God"[11] but only willingness to live in touch, to let presence be *peace of mind*.

Going with him past the dragon, however, means going with him through times when no effort seems availing to live in the presence of God, when God seems absent. I think of a conversation I once had with a Trappist brother about the words of Jesus on the cross, "My God, my God, why hast thou forsaken me?" Jesus was still in touch with God when he uttered that cry, the brother observed, but knew he was going to die and that God could never die. He felt the utter loneliness that human beings feel in the face of death, knowing we must die our own death, knowing we must die alone, feeling the contrast between "I am" and "I will die," between "I am" when I speak for God and "I will die" when I speak for myself. It is possible therefore for God to be far and near, far because I die and God lives, near because I am still in touch with the living God. I go with Christ past the dragon, according to this, when I am vulnerable to loneliness and yet hold to presence, when I am alone and yet unalone.

"No matter what form the dragon may take," Flannery O'Connor says, "it is of this mysterious passage past him, or into his jaws, that stories of any depth will always be concerned to tell." The many forms the dragon may take, I believe now, are the many images of desire, as desire moves restlessly from image to image, as I go from person to person, from place to place, from thing to thing, looking for someone, looking for something to fill and fulfill my life. It is indeed a "mysterious passage," I learned as I tried to make it on my second pilgrimage, for we are a mystery to ourselves, we feel God alone can fill our lives and yet each image we encounter is full of our own mystery for us, of dread and fascination. To meet the dragon is to be held transfixed and spellbound by an image, by someone or something I have invested with my desire, like a fleet-footed animal fascinated by the bright light of a lantern or a flashlight. To remember God then is to break the spell, to realize God is the true desire of my heart. It is as if the animal were to remember it is fleet-footed. I see the illusion, I remember God, and yet I do not act.

My mind is ready, but my heart is not yet ready. How may I go from restless desire to conscious love of God? "As a hart longs for flowing streams, so my soul longs for thee, O God. . . . My heart is ready, O God, my heart is ready!"[12] Here is where I want to be, longing for God, ready for God. It is a matter not only of mind but also of heart and soul. My mystery is my personal destiny, my purpose in life, my call from God. It is the answer to those three questions of Kant, "What can I know? What should I do? What may I hope?"[13] It is something I never finish knowing, never finish doing, never finish hoping as long as I live. When I meet someone or something that seems to embody that destiny, that purpose, that call, I meet with my own mystery in another. It is something to go beyond this reflection of me, to go on to the mystery of the other, to pass over to the other. When I come back again from that to my own mystery, then indeed I know, I do, I hope.

"Not that the study of his life, which was full and strong, upright and whole, rising and giving, yielded to me the secret of his heart," Massignon says of Al-Hallaj. "Rather it is he who fathomed mine and who probes it still."[14] I should say that too of passing over to others and coming back to myself, above all of passing over to Jesus and coming back from him to myself. My pilgrimage of heart was not a fathoming of hearts so much as a being fathomed in my own heart, but that, I found, is how I go from restless desire to conscious love of God. It is being known that leads to knowing, being loved that leads to loving. I had to give up the effort to know, the effort to love, and instead let myself be known and loved, be given the gift of knowledge and love. I had to go from striving to prayer. "Our relation to our fellow human beings is that of prayer," I learned from Kafka, "our relation to ourselves, that of striving," but I found I had to relate to myself as to another, to turn from striving to prayer in my relation to myself, and thus to let restless desire turn to unceasing prayer of the heart.

You don't really learn "the prayer of the heart," it seems, though I was learning to go from Christ in my mind to Christ in my heart on my pilgrimage of mind, and on to Christ praying in me on my pilgrimage of heart. You don't learn to long for God, I mean, you learn to become conscious of your longing. I think again of the spinning top, Nahman's image of the universe, to me an image of restless desire. It is in the unceasing movement of longing that I find *peace of heart*, in the top spinning, not in the top falling over, lying still and showing one of its four sides, one of the four Hebrew letters inscribed on a *dreidel*, *nun* or *gimel* or *he* or *shin*. These are like the many images that give expression to desire, one after another. "Not this, not this," I want to say to each definite image that comes up, but rather the spinning blur with the stability of a gyroscope. Peace is like that stability in movement, steadfast like "the heart of the world," always longing, always thirsting for the spring of water.

"I came . . . I forgot . . . I remembered. . . . "[15] These are the three stages on the journey described in the ancient Song of the Pearl and also, it seems, on the heart's journey to the eternal spring of water. "I came" to find the pearl, to drink of the spring. "I forgot" because of the illusions of the dragon; in fact I die, according to Nahman, or my soul dies within me, when I lose sight of the water, as I descend into the valley separating me from the spring. "I remembered" when I was reminded once again of the pearl; I revive, or my soul revives within me, when I am reminded once again of the water of life. These seem to be the stages, as I look back, on my last pilgrimage to Jerusalem, a coming, a forgetting, a remembering. I came, this time on a pilgrimage of soul, "upon the road of the union of love with God." I forgot what I was doing when I became caught up again in self, in my own loneliness, in "I am I," the autonomy of a self that relates only to itself. I remembered when I remembered God, when I began to live again for my soul, when I passed over from "I am I" and came back instead to "I am," a self inhabited by God.

There is something valid about this loneliness, though, this "I am I." It is by relating to myself and willing to be myself, as Kierkegaard says, that I am "grounded transparently"[16] in God. There is a passageway from "I am I" to "I am," and Jesus himself seems to go this way in his loneliness in the face of death. He seems thrown back upon himself when he cries, "My God, my God, why hast thou forsaken me?" Yet he moves again, even then, one last time, from loneliness into the presence of God, even in uttering these very words, in crying out to God. I am going with him then, when I go through my own loneliness into God's presence, as I did on each of my pilgrimages. As long as I am relating only to myself, I feel only the loneliness, but in the act of willing to be myself, of consenting to "I am," I do feel the presence, the transparent grounding. It is a presence, nevertheless, that does not take away loneliness, the sense of a God who is near and yet far, who does not take away my sense of myself.

"O alas, so long, so far!" I find *peace of soul* when I consent to God being far, to God being near, to God being far and near. For though God is far and near, I am one with Jesus in his relation with God. I am one soul, one spirit with him, for the Spirit dwelling in him is dwelling also in me. "If any, so by love refined, that he soul's language understood," John Donne says in "The Ecstasy," then he would understand the union of love:

> When love, with one another so
> Interinanimates two souls,
> That abler soul, which thence doth flow,
> Defects of loneliness controls. [17]

There is an "abler soul," he is saying, a soul formed of the union of two souls in love, and this one overshadows the loneliness of each soul in isolation, controls "defects of loneliness." He is speaking of man and woman in love, but it is true also of the love of God, "he who is united to the Lord becomes one spirit with him." [18] It is truer, in fact, "O alas, so long, so far!" is said of bodies in the poem, "Our bodies why do we forbear?"

Our bodies are the index of our souls, but if it is spirit in us that is longing and forbearing, and I take spirit to be mind and heart and soul, then the union is spiritual indeed, not an amalgam of souls, to be sure, but the one Spirit of God who is God's nearness even when God seems far away. Here is the paradox of loneliness. We are alone and yet unalone when we pass with Christ through loneliness, alone by ourselves, unalone with his Spirit in us. He too is alone and unalone, alone by himself, unalone with God's Spirit in him. "I in them and thou in me." I find a hint of this also in the Koran, in the chapter of Mary where Jesus says "Peace be upon me, the day I was born, and the day I die, and the day I am raised up alive!"[19] There is a peace upon him, and that peace, I want to say, comes upon everyone who enters into his relation with God, a peace of mind, a peace of heart, a peace of soul.

It is the human body, the "fleshly house of the soul," that is the home of the spirit, of the mind and the heart and the soul, but it is the body transfigured, the body risen, the body glorified. It is the body of Christ, "This is my body which is for you," or as David Daube interprets, This is me who am for you." When Jesus, risen from the dead, meets his disciples, he says, according to the Gospel of John, "Peace be with you."[20] I think again of the everyday greeting in Hebrew, *shalom aleichem*, and in Arabic, *salam alekum*, "Peace unto you" or "Peace be on you." I think then of what follows in the Gospel of John, "Receive the Holy Spirit." It is as if the everyday "Peace be with you" has broadened and deepened its meaning, with peace of mind, of heart, of soul, and has come to mean "Receive the Holy Spirit." The human body, as Charles Williams says in his essay, "The Index of the Body," is the index of a greater reality, "a whole being significant of a greater whole."[21] It is a whole being that conveys a greater whole, and that is what is happening when Jesus says "Peace be with you" and "Receive the Holy Spirit." A whole being is conveying the greater whole.

As I sat in the desert monastery, paging through the liturgical books, I came again and again upon the invocation of the Father and the Son and the Holy Spirit. I think now, as I look back into it, I must have been reading through the Divine Liturgy, as it is called, of Saint John Chrysostom. Anyway, the repeated naming of the Holy Trinity made me think of my efforts on these pilgrimages to speak of the Trinity to Jews and Muslims. Everything depends, I began to see, on the reality of the Holy Spirit, on the reality of this peace I had been finding. If "the Holy Spirit," *Ruach HaKodesh* in Hebrew, is simply "the general Hebraic term for enlightenment,"[22] simply the enlightenment of the spiritual person, that is, then the Holy Trinity fades from view, and there is God, only God, and Jesus, one of the many passing figures who cried out to God. If the Holy Spirit is an indwelling presence in us, on the other hand, then Jesus is alive and we can feel his life flowing in us.

I could feel life flowing there in the dawn at Mar Saba, as I looked out over the steep southern bank of the Kidron, and reading the words of the Trisagion Hymn, "Holy, holy, holy," in the book I was holding, I seemed to find words for it, words for a life that is stronger than death:

Agios o Theos,	Holy God,
agios ischyros,	holy mighty,
agios athanatos,	holy immortal,
eleison imas.	have mercy on us.[23]

Yes, it is a life stronger than death and loneliness, though it does not take away death, for I still must die someday, and loneliness, for I am still lonely for God, still lonesome for human beings. It is a life as terrible and as gentle, I think again, as the fire of the burning bush, that burns and does not consume. Melville in his diary speaks of "lonely monks"[24] at Mar Saba. I know what he means. Yet the still waters of loneliness flow deep with presence, the still waters of death flow deep with life.

There is the enlightenment of the spiritual person, the peace of mind, of heart, of soul I found, and that indeed can be called "the Holy Spirit," but there is a dimension of depth that goes beyond the understanding even of the spiritual person, "the peace of God, which passes all understanding"[25] and that, it seems to me, is truly the Holy Spirit, the presence that runs deeper than loneliness, the life that runs deeper than death. This is the peace I was glimpsing all along, it seems to me now, as I came to peace of mind, resting in presence of mind and letting it become presence of God, as I came to peace of heart, resting in the lonely longing of the heart and letting it become unceasing prayer, as I came to peace of soul, resting in God being far and near, going with Christ, that is, through loneliness to presence. "Peace I leave with you; my peace I give to you," Jesus says in the Gospel of John, after promising the Holy Spirit; "not as the world gives do I give to you."[26]

Here is the convergence point of the religions, the peace of God, the peace which is the gift of God, "not as the world gives." Yet it is the peace we also give to one another, like the Sabbath peace, *shabbat shalom* as everyone would say to one another on Friday afternoon as everything was closing in Jerusalem, or like the kiss of peace, the greeting we would give to one another every time at Eucharist, or like the handclasp and the kiss on the hand we gave to one another in the Sufi mosque in the Old City, after chanting and dancing and sharing mint tea. I feel the paradox of speaking of the peace of God at a time when religious wars are being fought all over the world. Still, it is the truth, it is possible to live in peace if we pass over to the mystery of God in one another and come back to the mystery of God in ourselves. The locus of peace, I believe, is in passing over, in going over to one another and coming back again to ourselves, in going deep in one another, in going deep in ourselves, in going through our death to God's life, in going through our loneliness to God's presence, in embracing mystery.

Notes

Prologue: The Homing Spirit

1. Cf. Dominique Lapierre, *The City of Joy*, tran. Kathryn Spink (Garden City, NY: Doubleday, 1985), p. 41, on the naming (Anand Nagar, City of Joy), and p. 101 on the name coming true.

2. John Henry Newman, *A Grammar of Assent* (Notre Dame and London: University of Notre Dame Press, 1979), p. 276.

3. Rom. 8:26.

4. "One man lives only for his own needs . . . [another] lives for his soul and remembers God." Leo Tolstoy, *Anna Karenina*, tran. Louise and Aylmer Maude (London: Oxford University Press, 1973), p. 411.

Chapter 1. A Pilgrimage of the Mind

1. Cf. my discussion of mediation in *A Search for God in Time and Memory* (New York: Macmillan, 1969), pp. 75–113, and in *Time and Myth* (Garden City, NY: Doubleday, 1973), pp. 70–81.

2. Matt. 27:46 and Mark 15:34. Here and throughout, unless otherwise indicated, I use the Revised Standard Version (RSV).

3. William Blake, "The Mental Traveler," in *The Complete Writings of William Blake*, ed. Geoffrey Keynes (London: Oxford University Press, 1966), p. 424.

4. Gal. 2:20.

5. William Morris, *The Well at the World's End*, vols. 18 and 19 in *The Collected Works of William Morris* (London: Longmans, 1910–15).

6. Stephen Graham, *With the Russian Pilgrims to Jerusalem* (London: Macmillan, 1913), p. 6.

7. Dante, *Paradiso* 3:85, in *Dante's Paradiso* tran. P. H. Wicksteed (London: J. M. Dent, 1958), p. 31.

8. Luke 19:42, in the King James Version (KJV).

9. 2 Chron. 32:31. David Daube uses the phrase "the test of loneliness" in discussing Hezekiah in his lecture "He That Cometh" (Cowley, Oxford: Church Army Press, 1966), p. 6.

10. Graham, *With the Russian Pilgrims to Jerusalem*, p. 3.

11. Exod. 3:3–4.

12. Dag Hammarskjold, *Markings*, tran. Leif Sjöborg and W. H. Auden (New York: Knopf, 1964), p. 89.

13. Martin Heidegger, *Being and Time*, tran. John Macquarrie and Edward Robinson (New York: Harper & Row, 1962); and *On Time and Being*, tran. Joan Stambaugh (New York: Harper & Row, 1972). The former was first published in German (*Sein und Zeit*) in 1927; the latter, first given as a lecture in 1962.

14. Al-Hallaj, quoted by Louis Massignon, "Time in Islamic Thought," in *Man and Time*, ed. Joseph Campbell (New York: Pantheon, 1957), p. 113.

15. Matt. 13:45–46. Cf. the medieval poem *Pearl*, tran. J. R. R. Tolkien, in *Sir Gawain and the Green Knight, Pearl, and Sir Orfeo* (Boston: Houghton Mifflin, 1975), pp. 89–122. Cf. also John Steinbeck, *The Pearl* (New York: Viking, 1947).

16. Massignon, "Time in Islamic Thought," p. 112.

17. Matt. 10:39.

18. Massignon, "Time in Islamic Thought," p. 114. I am quoting the phrase "a shock of grace" from Massignon and the phrase "a severe mercy" from a letter of C. S. Lewis to Sheldon Vanauken written on 8 May, 1955, and giving the title to Vanauken's story of his own loss, *A Severe Mercy* (New York: Harper & Row, 1977). Lewis perhaps took it from Augustine's *Confessions*, tran. Edward Pusey (1800–1882), bk. 8. In the copy I have (Franklin Center, PA: Franklin Library, 1982), p. 157.

19. Luke 24:5.

20. Marie Louise von Franz quotes this from a conversation with Jung in her preface to *Aurora Consurgens* tran. R. F. C. Hull and A. S. B. Glover (New York: Random House/Pantheon, 1966), p. xiii.

21. Massignon, "Time in Islamic Thought," p. 113.

22. Ludwig Wittgenstein, *Notebooks, 1914–1916*, tran. G. E. M. Anscombe (New York: Harper & Row, 1969), p. 74 (I have changed "man" to "one" as in the German on the facing page: *Nur wer nicht in der Zeit, sondern in der Gegenwart lebt, ist glücklich*).

23. Heidegger's preface to William J. Richardson, *Heidegger: Through Phenomenology to Thought* (The Hague: M. Nijhoff, 1963), p. xx (*die Lichtung des Sichverbergens*).

24. Massignon, "Time in Islamic Thought," p. 113.

25. Augustine, *Confessions* 10.16(Loeb Classical Library, tran. William Watts [Cambridge, MA: Harvard University Press, 1951], 2:117), where both the phrase "remember memory" (*memoriam memini*) and the phrase "remember forgetfulness" (*memini oblivionem*) are used.

26. John 16:22.

27. Matt. 26:32; Mark 14:28.

28. John 16:20, 21.

29. Luke 22:19; 1 Cor. 11:24.

30. William Shakespeare, Sonnets 30:2 and 107:2.

31. Eph. 3:17.

32. John 16:16.

33. C. S. Lewis, *Surprised by Joy* (San Diego, New York, London: Harcourt Brace Jovanovich, 1955), p. 18.

34. David Daube in his lecture "He That Cometh," p. 14, argues persuasively for "the bread of the Coming One" as the proper translation rather than "daily bread" in Matt. 6:11 and Luke 11:3. The other alternative, "supersubstantial bread," in the Latin translation of Matthew and in Origen's commentary on the Lord's Prayer, suggests to me "the bread from heaven" in John 6:32.

35. Matt. 5:3–10.

36. Søren Kierkegaard, *Philosophical Fragments*, tran. David Swenson and Howard V. Hong (Princeton, NJ: Princeton University Press, 1962), pp. 131, 71.

37. Heb. 11:1 (KJV).

38. Luke 23:46. Charles de Foucauld's meditation on this, his *prière d'abandon*, is in his *Écrits spirituels* (Paris: Gigord, 1951), p. 29. His words, "I am happy, and I lack nothing" (my translation) are on p. 233.

39. John 6:27.

40. Cf. Massignon's story as told by Herbert Mason in his foreword to the English edition of Louis Massignon, *The Passion of Al-Hallaj* (Princeton, NJ: Princeton University Press, 1982), 1:xxv. Cf. also Massignon's own preface, *ibid.*, 1:lxiii on the "witness of the instant" and the "Witness of the Eternal."

41. John 17:9.

42. Luke 20:38. Cf. Matt. 22:32 and Mark 12:27. Cf. my discussion in *The City of the Gods* (New York: Macmillan, 1965), pp. 22–23.

43. Matt. 5:34, 37. On Al-Hallaj, cf. my *Reasons of the Heart* (New York: Macmillan, 1978), p. 66 ("unity of witness") and p. 10 ("I am the truth").

44. Daube, "He That Cometh," p. 11 ("I am"), p. 8 (*Aphiqoman*), and p. 13 ("This is my body").

45. Kierkegaard defines these terms in *Fear and Trembling*, tran. Walter Lowrie (with *Sickness unto Death*) (Garden City, NY: Doubleday, Anchor, 1954), pp. 38–64. Cf. my discussion of hope and willingness in *The Reasons of the Heart*, p. 92.

46. John 6:20 (my translation), but also Matt. 14:27 and Mark 6:50. The "I am" sayings are often obscured in the translations "It is I" as here, and "I am he" as in John 4:26 and 8:28 and 18:5, where the original Greek has in each instance simply "I am."

47. Foucald, *Écrits spirituels*, p. 40 (my translation). This saying of Foucauld's is also quoted by Massignon in *The Passion of Al-Hallaj*, 3:73.

48. Hammarskjold, *Markings*, p. 86.

49. I am quoting from the first three of the Twelve Steps of Alcoholics Anonymous.

50. John 14:28 and 10:30.

51. Augustine, *Confessions* 1.1 Loeb Classical Library, p. 2; my translation of *inquietum est cor nostrum, donec requiescat in te*.

52. The title in English of Bach's Cantata no. 147. I quote and discuss it briefly in *The House of Wisdom* (San Francisco: Harper & Row, 1985), p. 3.

53. Hammarskjold, in his leaflet for the United Nations Meditation Room, "A Room of Quiet" (New York: United Nations, 1971), opening sentence. See my discussion of this sentence in *The Church of the Poor Devil* (New York: Macmillan, 1982), p. 156, and in *The House of Wisdom*, p. 4.

54. John 8:28 (my translation). Here, too, as n. 46 above, the "I am" saying can be obscured by the usual rendering "I am he," where the original has simply "I am."

Chapter 2. A Pilgrimage of the Heart

1. T. E. Lawrence, *Seven Pillars of Wisdom* (Harmondsworth, England: Penguin and Jonathan Cape, 1971), p. 364. Cf. my discussion of this passage in *The Reasons of the Heart* (New York: Macmillan, 1978), p. 1.

2. Martin Buber, *I and Thou*, tran. Ronald Gregor Smith (New York: Charles Scribner's Sons, 1958).

3. Luke 7:35.

4. Plato, *Symposium*, in *The Dialogues of Plato*, tran. Benjamin Jowett (New York: Random House, 1937), 1:331.

5. Matt. 11:19. Yet here too, it is noted in the RSV, "Other ancient authorities read *children*" as in Luke 7:35. Cf. Plato, *Symposium*, in *Dialogues of Plato*, 1:333, on mortal and immortal children.

6. Cf. the section entitled "The Restlessness of Desire," in Leo Bersani and Ulysse Dutoit, *The Forms of Violence* (New York: Schocken, 1985), pp. 110–25, and the references there to Freud on the "primary process."

7. Cf. E. R. Seary, *Place Names of the Avalon Peninsula of the Island of Newfoundland* (Toronto and Buffalo: University of Toronto, 1971), p. 58, where it is said to be "possibly named after a ship."

8. Franz Kafka, *The Great Wall of China*, tran. Willa and Edwin Muir (New York: Schocken, 1974), p. 150.

9. Cf. Milan Kundera, *Life is Elsewhere*, tran. Peter Kussi (New York: Knopf, 1974), who takes the title from a saying of Arthur Rimbaud (*La vie est ailleurs*).

10. John 1:1, 14.

11. Cf. Bernard Lonergan, *Verbum, Word and Idea in Aquinas* (Notre Dame: Notre Dame University Press, 1967).

12. Ignatius of Antioch, Epistle to the Romans, tran. Kirsopp Lake, *The Apostolic Fathers*, Loeb Classical Library (Cambridge, MA: Harvard University Press, 1952), 1:227 and 229.

13. Roland Barthes, *A Lover's Discourse*, tran. Richard Howard (New York: Hill and Wang, 1978), p. 1. Cf. my discussion of this in *The House of Wisdom* (San Francisco: Harper & Row, 1985), pp. 96 and 101.

14. Nahman of Bratslav, quoted by Arthur Green, *Tormented Master* (Tuscaloosa, AL: University of Alabama Press, 1979), p. 310.

15. Deut. 6:4.

16. Kafka, "Reflections on Sin, Pain, Hope, and the True Way," no. 101, in *The Great Wall of China*, p. 183. Willa and Edwin Muir translate: "Our relation to our fellow man is that of prayer, our relation to ourselves that of effort." I take the word "striving" from Nahum Glatzer's translation of the same passage in his *Language of Faith* (New York: Schocken, 1967), p. 35.

17. I make this distinction between the "things of life" and our "relation to the things" in my book *Time and Myth* (Garden City, NY: Doubleday, 1973), starting on pp. 12–14 and using it all through the book.

18. Cf. Robertson Davies, *At My Heart's Core* and *Overlaid*, Two Plays (Toronto: Clark, Irwin, 1966).

19. J. R. R. Tolkein, *The Lord of the Rings* (London: Allen and Unwin, 1969), p. 907.

20. Cant. 2:7; 3:5; and 8:4.

21. Cant. 5:2.

22. Wordsworth, "I grieved for Buonaparte," in *The Poems of William Wordsworth*, ed. Thomas Hutchinson (London: Oxford University Press, 1923), p. 304.

23. Robertson Davies, *Fifth Business* (Toronto: Macmillan, 1970), p. 305.

24. Cf. Abraham Heschel, *The Sabbath* (New York: Farrar, Straus & Giroux, 1951), pp. 48–62, on the Sabbath as bride and queen (theme of the hymn *Lechah Dodi*, p. 61).

25. Eccl. 3:5.

26. *Le paysage se reflète, s'humanise, se pense en moi*, quoted by Joachim Gasquet, *Cézanne* (Paris: Bernheime-Jeune, 1926), p. 132.

27. D. H. Lawrence, *The Man Who Died* (New York: Knopf, 1950), pp. 26–27.

28. Matt. 6:9–13; Luke 11:2–4; John 17.

29. Claude Lévi-Strauss, *Myth and Meaning* (New York: Schocken, 1979), p. 3.

30. Albert Camus, quoted by V. S. Pritchett, *The Turn of the Years* (the Chantry, Wilton, Salisbury, Wiltshire: Michael Russell, 1982), p. 46.

31. *Nahman of Bratslav: The Tales*, tran. Arnold J. Band (New York: Paulist Press, 1978), p. 269 (Cf. also the translation by Green, *Tormented Master*, p. 301).

32. Brhadaranyaka Upanishad 4.5.15, in Heinrich Zimmer, *The Philosophies of India*, ed. Joseph Campbell (New York: Pantheon, 1951), p. 363.

33. Cf. my discussion of the three movements of contemplation in *The House of Wisdom*, pp. 26–27. Here instead of "spiral" I say "oblique" as in Aquinas, *Summa Theologiae*, II–II, q. 180, a. 6.

34. Dag Hammarskjold, *Markings*, tran. Leif Sjöberg and W. H. Auden (New York: Knopf, 1964), p. 56.

35. Simone Weil, *Waiting for God*, tran. by Emma Craufurd (New York: Putnam, 1951), p. 135. Cf. my discussion of this saying of hers in *The House of Wisdom*, pp. 101–2.

36. Matt. 16:16, 18, 22, 23 (KJV).

37. Hammarskjold, *Markings*, p. 36.

38. *Nahman of Bratslav: The Tales*, p. 269.

39. Massignon, "Time in Islamic Thought," in *Man and Time*, ed. Joseph Campbell (New York: Pantheon, 1957), p. 114.

40. Plato, *Timaeus* 37d (my translation). Jowett translates "a moving image of eternity" in *The Dialogues of Plato*, 2:19. Cf. also A. E. Taylor, *A Commentary on Plato's Timaeus* (Oxford: Clarendon, 1928), p. 187, who says time derives from eternity for Plato as the numbers do from one.

41. Mark 1:35; Matt. 14:23; Luke 6:12.

42. Matt. 12:8; Mark 2:28; Luke 6:5.

43. John 5:17. Cf. Gen. 2:3.

44. Augustine, *Confessions* 13.36 vol. 2, p. 472 (my translation of *sabbato vitae aeternae requiescamus in te*). Cf. my discussion of this in *Time and Myth*, pp. 56–57.

45. Here and after the two following paragraphs I am quoting the last stanza of John Donne's last poem "An Hymn to God the Father"

as quoted by Izaak Walton, *Lives of Donne and Herbert*, ed. S. C. Roberts (Cambridge: At the University Press, 1957), p. 38.

46. A central passage in Nahman's teaching on *zimzum* is quoted by Green, *Tormented Master*, p. 311.

47. Mark 10:47 and 48; Luke 18:38 and 39. On "the prayer of the heart," cf. *Writings from the Philokalia on Prayer of the Heart*, tran. E. Kadloubovsky and G. E. H. Palmer (London: Faber and Faber, 1951) and also *The Way of the Pilgrim* cited in n. 52 below.

48. Matt. 15:14 (KJV).

49. Edith Stein, quoted by Romaeus Leuven in his preface to her autobiography, *Life in a Jewish Family*, tran. Josephine Koeppel (Washington, DC: Institute of Carmelite Studies, 1986), p. 2.

50. Quoted by Waltraud Herbstrith, *Edith Stein*, tran. Bernard Bonowitz (San Francisco: Harper & Row, 1985), p. 30.

51. Luke 11:1.

52. *The Way of a Pilgrim*, tran. R. M. French (New York: Seabury, 1965), esp. at the beginning of the second narrative, pp. 19–21.

53. Cf. Paul Flohr, "The Road to I and Thou," in *Texts and Responses*, Studies Presented to Nahum N. Glatzer, ed. Michael Fishbane and Paul Flohr (Leiden: Brill, 1975), pp. 201–25. The phrase "no more Thou in the I" is in Buber's introduction (1909) to his book *Ecstatic Confessions*, ed. Paul Flohr and tran. Esther Cameron (San Francisco: Harper & Row, 1985), p. 7.

54. Buber, *Ecstatic Confessions*, p. 1.

55. "Only the hand that erases. . . . " is quoted by Dag Hammarskjold as the epigraph to his diary *Markings*, p. 3. "When God laughs to the soul. . . . " is a paraphrase of a longer statement by Eckhart that I discuss in *The Reasons of the Heart*, p. 48.

56. John 17:23.

57. Buber, *I and Thou*, pp. 66–67. Cf. my discussion of this passage in *The House of Wisdom*, pp. 91–92.

58. Immanuel Kant, *Critique of Pure Reason*, tran. Norman Kemp Smith (London: Macmillan, 1963), p. 93.

59. Bernard Lonergan, *The Subject* (Milwaukee: Marquette University Press, 1968), p. 11.

60. Cant. 8:6.

61. The dictionary I was using is *Webster's Third New International Dictionary*.

62. Gert Hofmann, *The Parable of the Blind*, tran. Christopher Middleton (New York: Fromm, 1986), pp. 69–70. Cf. F. Grossman, *The Paintings of Bruegel* (London: Phaidon, 1966), pls. 147–51.

63. Cf. my discussion of Rouault's engraving in *The Church of the Poor Devil* (New York: Macmillan, 1982), pp. 65–66.

64. Nicholas of Cusa, *The Vision of God*, tran. Emma Gurney Salter (New York: Ungar, 1960). Cf. my discussion in *The Reasons of the Heart*, pp. 39–40.

65. Taha Husayn, *The Stream of Days*, tran. Hilary Wayment (Cairo: Al-Maaref, 1943), pp. 21–22. Cf. his first volume, *An Egyptian Childhood*, tran. E. H. Paxton (London: Routledge, 1932), p. 92, on blind sheikhs.

66. Bersani and Dutoit, *The Forms of Violence*, p. v.

67. Hammarskjold, *Markings*, p. 19.

68. Ps. 23:4.

69. Buber, *Good and Evil*, tran. Ronald Gregor Smith and Michael Bullock (New York: Charles Scribner's Sons, 1953), p. 43.

Interlude: Heart and Soul

1. Etty Hillesum, *Etty: A Diary 1941–43*, ed. J. G. Garlandt and tran. Arnold J. Pomerans (London: Jonathan Cape, 1983), p. 194.

2. Phil. 3:13–14 (KJV).

3. *The Cloud of Unknowing and Other Works*, tran. Clifton Wolters (New York: Penguin, 1980), p. 66.

4. Cf. my discussion of "the imagination of the heart" in my book *The House of Wisdom* (San Francisco: Harper & Row, 1985), p. 95.

5. Jean Giono, *The Man Who Planted Trees*, with an afterword by Norma L. Goodrich (Chelsea, VT: Chelsea Green, 1985), p. 25 (originally published in *Vogue* in 1954 as "The Man Who Planted Hope and Grew Happiness").

6. Ibid., p. 51.

7. Luke 21:19 (KJV).

8. Rev. 3:10 (cf. 6:1–8 on the Four Horsemen).

126 • The Homing Spirit

9. Norma L. Goodrich in Giono, *The Man Who Planted Trees*, p. 50.

10. *The Cloud of Unknowing* and Saint John of the Cross, *The Dark Night of the Soul*, in *The Cloud of Unknowing and Other Works*, pp. 46 and 34 respectively.

11. 1 John 4:18.

12. Kafka, *The Great Wall of China*, tran. Willa and Edwin Muir (New York: Schocken, 1974), p. 184 (No. 104).

13. A saying ascribed to the Buddha in the *Dhammapada* (no. 184), though the word used there, *tapo*, may mean "austerity" as S. Radakrishnan translates, *The Dhammapada* (Madras: Oxford University Press, 1984), p. 120, rather than "prayer." The modern word *tap* in Hindi, from the same root as *tapo* in Pali, can mean "heat" or "fever" (malaria) or "penance."

14. Søren Kierkegaard, *Purity of Heart Is to Will One Thing* tran. Douglas V. Steere (New York: Harper & Row, 1965).

15. Reiner Schürmann, *Meister Eckhart* (Bloomington: Indiana University Press, 1978), p. xiv.

16. From "Rules for the Discernment of Spirits," in *The Spiritual Exercises of Saint Ignatius* tran. John Morris (Westminster, MD: Newman, 1943), pp. 111–12.

17. Leo Bersani and Ulysse Dutoit, *The Forms of Violence* (New York: Schocken, 1985), p. 115.

18. René Girard, *"To double business bound"* (Baltimore: Johns Hopkins University Press, 1978), p. ix.

19. Maxim Gorky, *Reminiscences of Leo Nikolaevich Tolstoy* tran. S. S. Koteliansky and Leonard Woolf (New York: Huebsch, 1920), pp. 12–13.

20. John 4:24.

21. Elie Wiesel, *The Trial of God* (New York: Random House, 1979), pp. 63–64.

22. Gorky, *Reminiscences of Tolstoy*, p. 1.

23. J. R. R. Tolkien, *The Lord of the Rings* (London: Allen and Unwin, 1969), p. 971.

24. 1 Cor. 13:12 (KJV).

25. Martin Lings, *A Sufi Saint of the Twentieth Century* (Lahore, Pakistan: Suhail Academy, 1981), p. 210.

26. Isa. 26:8.

Chapter 3: A Pilgrimage of the Soul

1. Luke 20:38; Matt. 22:32; Mark 12:27; John 4:24.
2. Santa Teresa de Jesus, *Obras Completas*, vols., ed. Fr. Efren de la Madre de Dios (Madrid: La Editorial Catolica, 1954), 2:960 (my translation).
3. Mark 4:41. The words are inscribed on the gate of an orphanage for Arab girls designed by Conrad Schick and built in 1865, according to Martin Gilbert, *Jerusalem* (London: Hogarth, 1985), p. 123. It was torn down in 1980, according to Nitza Rosovsky, *Jerusalemwalks* (New York: Holt, Rinehart and Winston, 1982), p. 217. All that remains of it now is the gate with its inscription, and that is what I saw in 1985.
4. This is Edith Stein's *ceterum censeo*, as she called it, using Cato's phrase, according to Josephine Koeppel in her afterword to Edith Stein's autobiography, *Life in a Jewish Family* (Washington, DC: ICS Publications, 1986), p. 423.
5. Elie Wiesel, *Four Hasidic Masters and Their Struggle against Melancholy* (Notre Dame: University of Notre Dame Press, 1978), p. 16.
6. Thomas à Kempis, *The Imitation of Christ* 1.19 (tran. Leo Shirley-Price [New York: Penguin, 1952], p. 48).
7. John Donne, "Batter my heart, three-personed God." I quote here the copy I had with me at the time with its modernized spelling in *The Liturgy of the Hours* (New York: Catholic Book Publishing Company, 1975), 3:1974.
8. Nahum N. Glatzer, *Hillel the Elder* (New York: Schocken, 1966), p. 39. For the context of this saying see n. 23 below.
9. *Sayings of the Fathers (Pirke Aboth)* 1.14 (tran. Joseph H. Hertz [New York: Behrman, 1945], p. 25). It is also quoted and discussed by Glatzer, *Hillel the Elder*, partly on p. 32 and partly on p. 78. See also David Daube, "Wine in the Bible" (Cowley, Oxford: Church Army Press, 1974), p. 16, who says "it is not impossible that this motto includes an esoteric sense, 'If the Lord is not for me who is for me?'"
10. C. P. Cavafy, "Che Fece . . . Il Gran Rifiuto," in *Collected Poems*, tran. Edmund Keeley and Philip Sherrard, ed. George Savidis (London: Hogarth, 1984), p. 10.
11. John 9:9. KJV: "I am *he*"; italics mark the absence of the third

person pronoun in the Greek. "I am not" in John 18:17 and 25 corresponds to "I am" (again KJV: "I am *he*") in 18:5 and 6.

12. John 8:16; 8:29; 16:32; all in the KJV except "I and he who sent me," an alternative version of 8:16 in the RSV.

13. Cf. David Daube, *New Testament and Rabbinic Judaism* (London: Athlone, 1956), p. 328.

14. Cf. J. G. Fichte, *Science of Knowledge*, ed. and tran. Peter Heath and John Lachs (Cambridge: At the University Press, 1982), pp. 96 and 97, and G. W. F. Hegel, *The Phenomenology of Mind*, tran. J. B. Baillie (London: Macmillan, 1949), p. 219 (cf. also p. 679 and pp. 802–4). Cf. Søren Kierkegaard's critique of "I am I" in *Concluding Unscientific Postscript*, tran. David F. Swenson and Walter Lowrie (Princeton: Princeton University Press, 1941), pp. 107, 108, 169, 173, 176–77, and 179.

15. Cf. *Hoshanos: The Hoshana Prayers*, tran. and ed. Rabbi Avie Gold (Brooklyn, NY: Mesorah, 1980), pp. 84–85, where various interpretations are given. Note how the sentence is repeated, pp. 84, 90, 96, 104, and 106.

16. Robert Penn Warren, "John's Birches," a poem in the *New Yorker*, 12 August 1985, p. 26.

17. Al-Hallaj quoted by Mircea Eliade, *From Primitives to Zen* (London: Collins, 1967), p. 524.

18. Louis Massignon, *The Passion of Al-Hallaj*, tran. Herbert Mason (Princeton: Princeton University Press, 1982), 1:lv.

19. Martin Buber, *I and Thou*, tran. Ronald Gregor Smith (New York: Charles Scribner's Sons, 1958), p. 85.

20. Immanuel Kant, *Critique of Pure Reason*, tran. Norman Kemp Smith (London: Macmillan, 1963), p. 141.

21. Ursula LeGuin, *A Wizard of Earthsea* (Berkeley, CA: Parnassus, 1968), p. 185. Cf. my discussion of this in *The House of Wisdom* (San Francisco: Harper & Row, 1985), p. 13.

22. See my discussion of Newton's "sensorium of God" and Kant's human sensorium and Einstein's relativity in *The City of the Gods* (New York: Macmillan, 1965), p. 207.

23. Both of these sayings of Hillel are placed in the context of the rejoicing that takes places on the second night of the feast of Tabernacles at the ceremony of water-drawing. They are quoted in the Baby-

lonian Talmud in Sukkah 53a. I am quoting from *Sukkah*, tran. Israel
W. Slotki (London: Soncino, 1984), in the Hebrew-English *Babylonian
Talmud*, ed. Isidore Epstein (London: Soncino, 1960–1985), vol. 2:6,
p. 105. The corresponding saying of Jesus on the feast of Tabernacles
is John 7:34 (note also the water imagery in 7:37).

24. Al-Hallaj, quoted by Eliade, *From Primitives to Zen*, p. 524.

25. See the color reproduction in David and Tamara Talbot Rice,
Icons and Their History (Woodstock, NY: Overlook Press, 1974), pl. 8,
after p. 100, and the comment by Tamara Talbot Rice on p. 135, where
she points out that the cataloguers of the Tretyakov Gallery's icons take
the central figure to symbolize Christ, the one on his right to symbolize
God, and the one on his left to symbolize the Holy Spirit.

26. Abraham laughs, Gen. 17:17; Sarah laughs, Gen. 18:12 (and
protests that she has not, 18:15), and Isaac is named for laughter,
Gen. 21:6. Cf. above, chap. 2, n. 55, for Eckhart on laughter.

27. William Vaughn Moody, "The Death of Eve," in *The Poems and
Plays of William Vaughn Moody* (Boston and New York: Houghton Mif-
flin, 1912), 1:445. Cf. my discussion of this in *The Church of the Poor
Devil* (New York: Macmillan, 1982), pp. 21–22.

28. T. S. Eliot, "Burnt Norton," in *Four Quartets* (San Diego, New
York, London: Harcourt Brace Jovanovich, 1971), p. 14.

29. Cf. The Sermon on the Mount in Matt. 5-7. Matt. 6:23. "if
thine eye be evil" (KJV); "if your eye is not sound" (RSV). Cf. Matt.
20:15: "Is thine eye evil, because I am good?" (KJV). Also Mark 7:22:
"an evil eye" (KJV) and "envy" (RSV).

30. Martin Heidegger as quoted by Reiner Schürmann in the epigraph of his book *Meister Eckhart* (Bloomington, IN: Indiana University Press, 1978), p. vii.

31. Gen. 1:3. Cf. Gen. 1:10, 12, 18, 21, 25 ("And God saw that it
was good"), and 31 ("very good").

32. John 17:9.

33. Michael Polanyi, *The Tacit Dimension* (Garden City, NY: Doubleday, 1966), p. 4. Cf. my discussion of this in *Time and Myth* (Garden
City, NY: Doubleday, 1973), pp. 109–17.

34. Daube, *Wine in the Bible*, p. 16 (speaking of 1 Cor. 11:24). He
speaks here also of the parallel with Hillel's question, "If I am not for
myself. . . . "

35. Monica Strauss, *Leonardo da Vinci* (Mt. Vernon, NY: Artist's Limited Edition, 1984), p. 5.

36. Cf. my discussion of Leonardo and "light-bearing eyes" in *The House of Wisdom*, p. 107.

37. Cf. Jeanne Vronskaya, *Young Soviet Film Makers* (London: Allen & Unwin, 1972), pp. 33–35, on Andrei Tarkovsky and this film on Rublev. I saw the film in Berkeley at the Pacific Film Archive Theatre on 8 February 1987 when I was writing this chapter.

38. André Malraux, *Anti-Memoirs*, tran. Terence Kilmartin (New York: Bantam, 1970), p. 194. Cf. my discussion of this in *The Way of All the Earth* (New York: Macmillan, 1972), p. 168.

39. Here I am quoting from "Rules for the Discernment of Spirits," in *The Spiritual Exercises of Saint Ignatius*, tran. John Morris (Westminster, MD: Newman, 1943), p. 113 (cf. the earlier quotation above in the Interlude, p. 72).

40. John 5:19.

41. John 16:8.

42. A versicle and response in *The Liturgy of the Hours*, 3:931.

43. Miguel de Cervantes Saavedra, *Don Quixote*, tran. J. M. Cohen (Harmondsworth, Middlesex, England: Penguin, 1952), p. 54 ("I know who I am"), p. 434 ("I know certainly that I am enchanted"), p. 938 ("I was mad, but I am sane now").

44. John 3:8.

45. 1 John 3:2.

46. Buber, *I and Thou*, tran. Ronald Gregor Smith (New York: Charles Scribner's Sons, 1958), p. 11.

47. Erik Erikson, *The Life Cycle Completed* (New York and London: Norton, 1985), p. 41.

48. Ibid., pp. 40–41 and p. 88, where he is quoting Num. 6:26 (on the pronouns, cf. pp. 87–88). Cf. his essay "The Galilean sayings and the sense of 'I,'" *Yale Review*, Spring 1981, pp. 321–62.

49. John 14:6; 6:35; 11:25.

50. Erikson, *The Life Cycle Completed*, p. 40.

51. 1 John 1:1.

52. Mark 14:36.

53. Herman Melville, *Clarel*, ed. Walter E. Bezanson (New York: Hendricks, 1960), p. 228.

Epilogue: The Home of the Spirit

1. Christopher Smart, *Song to David*, (1763; reprint, Oxford: Clarendon, 1926), st. 40, p. 11.

2. *Othello*, act 1, sc. 1, line 65, and 1 Cor. 15:10.

3. Immanuel Kant, *Grounding for the Metaphysics of Morals*, tran. James W. Ellington (Indianapolis, IN: Hackett, 1981), p. 39.

4. Flannery O'Connor, *Mystery and Manners* (New York: Farrar, Straus & Giroux, 1969), p. 35.

5. This is John Henry Newman's translation (The Protocatechesis, par. 16) in *St. Cyril of Jerusalem's Lectures on the Christian Sacraments*, ed. F. L. Cross (London: SPCK, 1951), p. 50 (this is a quite literal version of the Greek on p. 10).

6. Albert Schweitzer, *The Quest of the Historical Jesus*, tran. W. Montgomery (New York: Macmillan, 1964), pp. 370–71. René Girard, *The Scapegoat* (Baltimore: Johns Hopkins University Press, 1986).

7. Matt. 28:20.

8. Luke 20:38. Cf. Robert S. Hartmann's introduction to Hegel, *Reason in History* (Indianapolis, IN: Bobbs-Merrill, 1953), pp. xxx–xl, on the four types of figures in history.

9. John 17:1.

10. John 13:3.

11. Cf. my discussion of Brother Lawrence (Nicholas Herman) and "the practice of the presence of God" in *The House of Wisdom* (San Francisco: Harper & Row, 1985), pp. 62–65.

12. Ps. 42:1 and 108:1.

13. Cf. my discussion of Kant's three questions in *The City of the Gods*, (New York: Macmillan, 1965), p. 217.

14. Louis Massignon, *The Passion of Al-Hallaj*, tran. Herbert Mason (Princeton: Princeton University Press, 1982), 1:lxv.

15. The Song of the Pearl is translated by S. G. Hall in *Gnosis*, ed. Werner Foerster (Oxford: Clarendon, 1972), 1:355–58 ("I came . . ." [p. 356]; "I forgot . . . " [p. 356]; "I remembered . . . " [p. 357]).

16. Cf. my discussion of Kierkegaard's formula of self-relation in *The Church of the Poor Devil* (New York: Macmillan, 1982), p. 127.

17. John Donne, "The Extasie," in *John Donne*, ed. John Hayward

(Harmondsworth, Middlesex, England: Penguin, 1969), pp. 56 and 57 (I have modernized the spelling).

18. 1 Cor. 6:17 (note how "one spirit" in this verse parallels "one flesh" in the verse before).

19. Koran 19:34, *The Koran Interpreted*, tran. Arthur J. Arberry (Oxford and New York: Oxford University Press, 1979), p. 305. Cf. my discussion of this verse in *The House of Wisdom*, p. 36. Cf. also Geoffrey Parrinder, *Jesus in the Qu'ran* (London: Faber & Faber, 1965), p. 28.

20. John 20:19 and 21.

21. Charles Williams, *The Image of the City and Other Essays* (London: Oxford University Press, 1958), p. 81.

22. Aryeh Kaplan, *Meditation and Kabbalah* (York Beach, ME: Samuel Weiser, 1982), p. 11.

23. *The Divine Liturgy*, ed. N. Michael Vaporis (Brookline, MA: Holy Cross Orthodox Press, 1983), p. 6. I found afterwards that Saint John of Damascus who was a monk at Mar Saba in the eighth century has a letter on the Trisagion Hymn where he argues the hymn is addressed not just to the Son but to Father and Son and Holy Spirit as is, he thinks, the "Holy, holy, holy" of Isa. 6:3. Cf. *Patrologia Graeca*, vol. 95, ed. P. Michaelis Lequien (Paris: Migne, 1864), pp. 24A and 25A.

24. Melville's diary on Mar Saba is quoted by Bezanson in his introduction to Melville's poem *Clarel*, p. xxv (part 3 of the poem is entitled "Mar Saba"). There were sixty-five monks when Melville was there, only nine when I was there.

25. Phil. 4:7.

26. John 14:27.